10397

Hau

# EXHIBIT DESIGN 4

# EXHIBIT DESIGN 4

Robert B. Konikow

**PBC** INTERNATIONAL, Inc.

GLEN COVE, NEW YORK

*Distributor to the book trade in the United States and Canada:*

**Rizzoli International Publications, Inc.**
300 Park Avenue South
New York, NY 10010

*Distributor to the art trade in the United States:*

**Letraset USA**
40 Eisenhower Drive
Paramus, NJ 07652

*Distributor to the art trade in Canada:*

**Letraset Canada Limited**
555 Alden Road
Markham, Ontario L3R 3L5, Canada

*Distributed throughout the rest of the world by:*

**Hearst Books International**
105 Madison Avenue
New York, NY 10016

**Library of Congress Cataloging-in-Publication Data**

Konikow, Robert B.
    Exhibit design 4 / by Robert B. Konikow.
       p.    cm.
    ISBN 0-86636-131-6
    1. Exhibits    I. Title.    II. Title: Exhibit design four.
    T396.5.K653    1990
    659.1'52—dc20               90-6924
                                CIP

Color separation, printing, and binding by
**Toppan Printing Co. (H.K.) Ltd. Hong Kong**
Typography by Jeanne Weinberg Typesetting

10 9 8 7 6 5 4 3 2 1

# Table
# of
# Contents

**INTRODUCTION**    9
**FOREWORD**    11

CHAPTER  **1**
**Small Exhibits**    13

CHAPTER  **2**
**Medium Exhibits**    59

CHAPTER  **3**
**Large Exhibits**    93

CHAPTER  **4**
**Giant Exhibits**    117

CHAPTER  **5**
**Multi-Level Exhibits**    131

CHAPTER  **6**
**Special Areas**    155

CHAPTER  **7**
**Museums**    183

CHAPTER  **8**
**Too Good To Leave Out**    207

**INDEX**    249

# INTRODUCTION

Robert B. Konikow

**A**s always, it is a rewarding experience to see the output of today's exhibit designers, to admire their technique, their imagination, their creativity. It is not a simple task to select some and reject others. Some of the decisions that are part of the process of selection may seem arbitrary, especially by those who are disappointed at not having their work included, and indeed, some of them are indeed arbitrary. There are no hard and fast criteria that permit one to say that, once an obvious level of professionalism has been reached, one entry is clearly superior to another.

**T**here are limits, of course, imposed by the quality of the illustrations sent in. Of all promotional media, the trade show or museum exhibit is the most difficult to photograph. It is a medium designed to be three-dimensional, to be a stage within which action is taking place. It takes place in a location where other installations, often part of a complex background, are competing for attention. It is hard to capture on two-dimensional film, especially during the limited time and the great activity of a trade show exposition. Yet things are improving. There has been a noticeable increase of photographic quality in the years since the first volume of this series appeared.

We have tried, in making our selection, to present as any different ideas and design approaches as possible, in an effort to expose a wide variety of techniques and of solutions to problems. In doing this, we have sometimes found it necessary to reject one entry, not because it lacked merit, but simply because it was too close to another already selected and written up. We have tried to include a wide variety of industries represented, and of geographical sources.

Finally, I'd like to make a comment on credits. The information given about each project is obtained from the individual or company which made the original submission. We can take no responsibility for the accuracy of the information that was given to us in the entry form. In particular, this applies to the listing of the individual or individuals credited with design. Many companies listed some such phrase as "In-house design" or "Designed by staff" in the space given for designer credit. However, in a book devoted to design, we felt it only right to credit the individual or individuals chiefly responsible, and made a special request for this information. When it was not forthcoming, we made the decision to omit that credit line. It is a controversial decision, and we wonder what would be most useful to the readers and users of this book.

In completion, it has been a rewarding experience to see all the entries that have been sent in from designers and exhibit houses all over the world, and by now, I feel that some of these people, even though I have never met them, have become old friends. Thank you all for your help.

CHAPTER

# 1

# SMALL
# EXHIBITS

**EXHIBITOR**
Murphy & Orr Co.
**PRODUCER**
Murphy & Orr Co.,
Forest Park, GA
**DESIGNER**
Jeff Raflo

New construction materials and techniques combine with a rich blend of the contemporary and traditional for an unusual design statement. Simple brass laminated framing with Rollerboard panels painted in Zolatone provides a lightweight, easily assembled exhibit. The entire back wall is a back-lit, silk screened translucent blueprint with a neon script title. The frameless showcases provide uninterrupted viewing of the models and the back wall, and the accenting cabinetry reinforces the exhibit geometry, while providing the required storage.

**EXHIBITOR**
Watson Bowman Acme
**PRODUCER**
Design for Industry Inc.,
   Buffalo, NY
**DESIGNERS**
Jack Snyder, Greg Meadows

Using many of the exhibitor's products as elements of the exhibit attracted an audience of architects and engineers. Black compression seals create obvious breaks on the detail counter and back wall of the exhibit, while the overhead truss that supports the lights is a section of the company's sinusoidal anchorage extrusion. When space permits, a clear acrylic model of a bridge bearing, edgelit with neon, is included with a conference table featuring another of the company's expansion joints embedded in its top.

**EXHIBITOR**
J.M. Pedreira & Son Inc.
**PRODUCER**
Escaparates Inc., Rio Piedras,
   Puerto Rico
**DESIGNER**
Wanda I. Nieves

Shown here in an 8'x30'
configuration, the display can be
used in 20' or 10' sizes. The
central bank's transparencies
provide Impact, while the
elegant cases display hardware
fixtures as if they were pieces of
jewelry.

**EXHIBITOR**
Taurus International
**PRODUCER**
Presentations South Inc.,
   Orlando, FL
**DESIGNERS**
Robert McGarry and
Tom Holman

Almost 50 models of pistols were
available for inspection by
visitors, in a booth whose design
did not overwhelm the product.
A small closing room, at the end
of the booth, was supplied for
meeting with dealers.

**EXHIBITOR**
Focusrite
**PRODUCER**
Dimension Works Inc.,
    Bensenville, IL
**DESIGNER**
Bill Hoffmockel

Focusrite needed a booth that would project a sophisticated corporate image to its potential clients in the classical music recording industry. Classic architectural elements achieved an elegant booth environment. The large centrally-located photomural showed the equipment installed, while actual components were shown on either side.

**EXHIBITOR**
Rodem Company
**PRODUCER**
The Alley Shop, Cincinnati, OH
**DESIGNER**
Barry Hatter

Based on Easy 2 elements, this 10' display for a distributor of electric components used a blow-up of a photo already familiar to clients and prospects because of its use in Rodem literature. An interesting visual effect was the continuous strip of clear plexiglass, painted blue on the back and adhered with Velcro to the display. It started at the right upper edge of the photomural and ran along the end cap to meet the matching blue inlay in the custom carpet, and picked up again on the podium in the front of the booth. The display came in at about $4,500, including the graphics, carpet and carrying bag, clear plexiglass table and chairs. The back wall and podium fit into four Easy 2 cases.

**EXHIBITOR**
Ecolab, Int'l. Division
**PRODUCER**
Kitzing Inc., Chicago, IL
**DESIGNER**
Ben Vargas

The centerpiece of this display is a revolving globe on which the countries with distribution are highlighted.

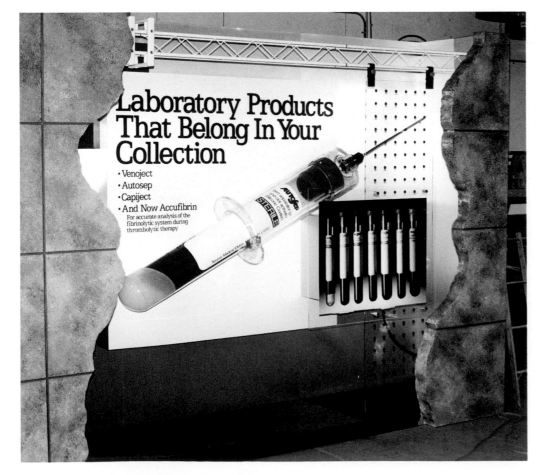

**EXHIBITOR**
Terumo Corp.
**PRODUCER**
Design for Industry, Buffalo, NY
**DESIGNERS**
Jack Snyder, Andrea Bilias,
    Tim Dexter, Greg Meadows

The exhibitor, with seven divisions, attends a number of shows in the health care industry. The "faux stone" backwall suggests corporate strength, while product graphics become three-dimensional statements relative to product positioning. Larger than life models, edge-lit acrylic, special recessed indirect lighting and layered photos add special emphasis and attract attention to product graphics.

**EXHIBITOR**
Wagner/Belden
**PRODUCER**
Kitzing Inc., Chicago, IL
**DESIGNER**
Ben Vargas

The exhibit design provides strong product graphics and modular components for varied space configurations. Selling stations permit sales staff to demonstrate and develop leads.

**EXHIBITOR**
**HBO & Co.**
**PRODUCER**
**Design South Inc., Atlanta, GA**
**DESIGNER**
**Joel Katzowitz**

The use of triangular shapes
throughout this island exhibit—
down to the custom-made carpet
—calls attention to the corporate
logo.

**EXHIBITOR**
Regal Ware Inc.
**PRODUCER**
KMK Industries Inc.,
    Milwaukee, WI
**DESIGNER**
Jack Wegner

Lumenyte, a flexible material that looks like neon, was used around the large transparencies and on the end returns, giving a modern enhancement to the exhibit area. The stand-alone module in the center, using fluorescent lighting to highlight featured products, brought the company name up front for greater visibility.

**EXHIBITOR**
McGard
**PRODUCER**
Giltspur Exhibits/Rochester,
    Rochester, NY
**DESIGNER**
David Uzarowski

This exhibit was designed to reflect the strength and security of the product—automotive wheel locks. The illuminated logo, with edge-lit plexi, projects a strong corporate image.

**EXHIBITOR**
Nichols-Homeshield
**PRODUCER**
Windsor Exhibits Inc., Elgin, IL
**DESIGNER**
James Gallagher

The product line was an assortment of architectural products that looked very unimpressive by themselves. Order was imposed by using an enlarged schematic drawing on clear plastic, on which actual parts were mounted in their correct positions. This gave meaning to each of the parts and related them to the main interest of show visitors.

**EXHIBITOR**
Rochester Instrument Systems
**PRODUCER**
Ontario Design Inc.,
    Rochester, NY
**DESIGNER**
Thomas Finn

The problem of displaying a large number of small products and components was solved by utilizing pedestals with translucent tops lit from beneath. The components were placed on individual plexiglass stands, with the other product shown on the back wall. A 10' tower with rotating company identification made for rapid recognition.

**EXHIBITOR**
Inter-Continental Hotels
**PRODUCER**
Convention Exhibits Inc.,
   Chicago, IL
**DESIGNERS**
Jack Reese, Michael Saubert

The focal point of this exhibit, designed to emphasize elegance, was a large, animated globe. LED lights showed the locations of the 130 members of the chain.

**EXHIBITOR**
Williams, Jackson, Ewing
**PRODUCER**
Adler Display Inc.
**DESIGNERS**
Ron Adler, Scott Mayer

This small booth was made to seem larger with the open work partitions that separate the two small conference rooms from the reception area. Two light boxes face the aisle to attract the attention of passers-by.

**EXHIBITOR**
Reggie's Wax
**PRODUCER**
Rogers Displays, Gardena, CA
**DESIGNERS**
Guy L'Esperance

Reggie Jackson's personal collection of antiques lends interest to the marketing of a product.

**EXHIBITOR**
Morgan Doors
**PRODUCER**
Hartwig Exhibitions,
    Milwaukee, WI
**DESIGNER**
G.P. Lyons

Note the unusual use of the product as part of the perimeter of this island exhibit.

**EXHIBITOR**
Sandridge Gourmet
**PRODUCER**
Joan Carol Design and Exhibit
    Group, Clinton, MD
**DESIGNER**
Alane Epperson

The exhibit uses three Instant display systems with marble-look panels. With a shallow back wall, there is ample room to demonstrate the actual fixtures that Sandridge places in the field.

**EXHIBITOR**
Reader's Digest
**PRODUCER**
1220 Exhibits Inc., Nashville, TN
**DESIGNER**
Miriam Owen

The exhibitor chose a classical custom environment, rendered in Williamsburg colors, showcasing its quality print publications and home video service.

**EXHIBITOR**
Inland Steel
**PRODUCER**
Kitzing Inc., Chicago, IL
**DESIGNERS**
James Hanlon, Fred Kitzing

Designed for a technical
conference on the Super
Collider, it was made of the
exhibitor's sheet steel, textured
with surface grinding. The dry
marker board, in the center,
invited physicists to use the
booth to discuss qualities of
steel, and to write formulas.

**EXHIBITOR**
South Central Bell
**PRODUCER**
Murphy & Orr Co.,
    Forest Park, GA
**DESIGNER**
George Stough, Stough &
Williams Design Consultant

Computer generated graphics,
installed in Outline frames,
creatively unify the varying
elements of the large
background illustrations.

**EXHIBITOR**
RCA Records, Country Music
    Division
**PRODUCER**
1220 Exhibits Inc., Nashville, TN
**DESIGNER**
Mark Meagher

To give visitors at public shows
the chance to meet the
company's artists, the counter
keeps fans from crowding in on
their objectives, while the
overhead monitors hold
continuous-play music videos.

**EXHIBITOR**
Jerry Madison Jewelry
**PRODUCER**
1220 KPW Productions,
  New York, NY
**DESIGNER**
Picmai

The elegant simplicity of this
booth and its open structure
attract passers-by, but also offers
a surprising amount of space for
salesmen's conferences.

**EXHIBITOR**
Sony-Cetek Inc.
**PRODUCER**
John Oldham Studios,
    Wethersfield, CT
**DESIGNER**
James L. Colbert

In a 10'x30' space, the exhibitor required a projected audio-visual presentation, individual product demo areas, and closet storage. The two central columns contained doors leading to generous storage space. The headers attached to these columns provided identity and hid tracklighting which washed the back wall. On the far right of the booth, a projector and rear screen was installed.

**EXHIBITOR**
Art-Craft Optical Co.
**PRODUCER**
Ontario Design Inc.,
    Rochester, NY
**DESIGNER**
Thomas Finn

A clean, crisp presentation: a central tower increases visibility while four connected vertical members unify the space. Set up and dismantling is quick, with low drayage and shipping costs.

**EXHIBITOR**
Caribbean Lumber Co.
**PRODUCER**
Exhibitgroup Atlanta, Atlanta, GA
**DESIGNER**
Mark S. Burns

The floor is an essential part of this display, since it is made of the product being promoted at the exhibit. Photos of the lumber in use are shown on the rear wall.

**EXHIBITOR**
Santander Federal Savings Bank
**PRODUCER**
Escaparates Inc., Rio Piedras,
    Puerto Rico
**DESIGNER**
Wanda I. Nieves

The diagonal header lends distinction to this small space, making it seem roomier. The bi-level computer desk rests on a golden column, and the monitor, sitting in a column with an attractive curved front, is easily seen from the aisle.

**EXHIBITOR**
W.A. Lane Inc.
**PRODUCER**
Exhibit Systems of California,
    Culver City, CA
**DESIGNER**
Jack Hejka

Using a combination of Nimlok, Nimlink, and brushed aluminum laminate panels, this interesting layout places video monitors inside columns on either side of the display, and has a conference room enclosed with smoked plexiglass windows.

**EXHIBITOR**
Bearings Inc.
**PRODUCER**
Promotional Fixtures Inc.,
    Rittman, OH
**DESIGNER**
Keith L. Gamble

These modular units, with built-in casters, simply roll out of their shipping cases and into position. The entire exhibit uses five totally assembled modules, resulting in minimal installation and dismantling labor and effort.

**EXHIBITOR**
Pueringer Distributing Inc.
**PRODUCER**
ABF Industries, St. Paul, MN
**DESIGNER**
Jerry Broberg

The exhibitor was moving into larger space, and thought he needed a custom booth, but this modular design based on Nimlink elements filled the bill. It could be figured into 10' and 20' units, as well as the 30' size shown here. It takes just three hours to set up.

**EXHIBITOR**
Universal Motors
**PRODUCER**
The Display Shop, Dale, WI
**DESIGNER**
Jon Horn

To romanticize the product —boat motors—blue sails and port hole transparencies graced the background. The pedestals for the 600-pound motors were the crates in which they were shipped, allowing ease of transport and cutting down on rigger costs at the show. The planter box in the center softened the crisp effect of the display, serving as demarcation for a small conference area.

**EXHIBITOR**
Fitness Quest
**PRODUCER**
Communication Exhibits Inc.,
    Canal Fulton, OH
**DESIGNER**
Brian Walters

Although this 20' space contains both a demonstration platform and a private conference room, the shallow back wall and the quiet color pattern keeps it from becoming crowded. The truss adds rigidity to the structure.

**EXHIBITOR**
Redkin Hair Products
**PRODUCER**
Exhibit Systems of California,
    Culver City, CA
**DESIGNER**
Larry Carder

This exhibit was composed of three 10' Nimlink displays positioned in an L-shaped peninsula. The panels, of 1/2'' opaque white plexiglass, were cut into iceberg shapes and connected with Nimlink extrusions. A Nimlink table with a custom countertop created a small product demonstration area. The entire display packed into two wooden crates.

**EXHIBITOR**
Canyon Products
**PRODUCER**
Communication Exhibits Inc.,
   Canal Fulton, OH
**DESIGNER**
David Jeffries

Because of its modularity, this
exhibit can easily be extended or
converted to an island display.
The custom-made wheel rack,
on the left, allows prospects to
select the tire they need for their
wheel chairs.

**EXHIBITOR**
Monsanto
**PRODUCER**
The Robert Falk Group,
    St. Louis, MO
**DESIGNERS**
Robert J. Falk Jr., Steven Harrison

A series of individual segments, each illustrating a specific use of industrial coatings, produced a very flexible exhibit. This permitted each visitor to quickly find the product that interested him. Varied-colored pillars attracted a lot of attention.

**EXHIBITOR**
Virgin Atlantic Airways
**PRODUCER**
Giltspur Exhibits/Rochester,
 Rochester, NY
**DESIGNER**
Dirk Hass

The cut-out shape of an airplane gains attention by being mounted just away from a light-washed wall. The transparencies also garner attention from their rear-lit mounting. Note the use of actual airplane seats in the booth.

**EXHIBITOR**
Dimension Works Inc.
**PRODUCER**
Dimension Works Inc.,
    Bensenville, IL
**DESIGNER**
Bill Hoffmockel

This 20' x 20' booth features a
stair-stepped soffit ring of satin
aluminum with pierce-cut and
internally illuminated identity.
Each of the four modules
supporting the soffit outlines a
different category of products
and services. The center kiosk
contains animated display areas
with sequential lighting which
appears and disappears through
two-way mirrors, giving the
appearance of holograms.

**EXHIBITOR**
Seiko Instruments
**PRODUCER**
Color & Design Exhibit Inc.,
    Portland, OR

A series of free-standing,
demonstration kiosks allow a
variety of configurations. The
kiosk ceilings give some
protection from ambient light.

**EXHIBITOR**
Rampart Packaging
**PRODUCER**
Beyond Exhibits Inc.,
    Newport News, VA
**DESIGNER**
Teddie Jo Ryan

Large transparencies show
product, while there is shelf
space for actual samples.

**EXHIBITOR**
Dickinsons/Lost Acres
**PRODUCER**
The Display Shop, Dale, WI
**DESIGNER**
Rusty Mothes

These two exhibits were
designed to go together, as both
companies usually exhibit at the
same shows, and both are
divisions of Smucker's Jam. Set
up back to back, Lost Acres
employs a country kitchen,
Dickinson's a dining room with
both using turn-of-the-century
themes. Appropriate antiques are
incorporated among the product
displays.

**EXHIBITOR**
Karp's Bakery Products
**PRODUCER**
Dimension Works Inc.,
    Bensenville, IL
**DESIGNER**
Susan Kemble

The central structure incorporates ovens for baking, storage facilities, and counters for sampling the product. The outer corner modules incorporate larger-than-life product transparencies and a chase-light identity sign.

**EXHIBITOR**
Metal Leve
**PRODUCER**
Cyclonics Inc., Medina, OH
**DESIGNER**
Ricardo Rizzini

Designed to introduce a Brazilian company into the United States, this exhibit uses large transparencies to show the size and stability of the company. Cases and shelves show its broad range of capabilities.

**EXHIBITOR**
Rasna
**PRODUCER**
Exhibitgroup San Francisco,
    South San Francisco, CA
**DESIGNER**
Jayne Beetlestone

New finishes and industrial fittings give this island exhibit an appropriate technical look. High-mounted monitors extend the demonstrations beyond the people seated at the keyboards.

**EXHIBITOR**
Seagil Software
**PRODUCER**
Atlanta Display Mart, Atlanta, GA
**DESIGNER**
Susan Burns

This 20' x 20' island display used Nimlink elements and Zero trusses to produce the decorative elements, while the demonstration tables were custom designed. Using a single Zero truss leg furnished more leg room for sit-down presentations of the computer programs. The 94" x 34" name signs held 1/2" white plexiglass letters glues to clear panels, and were suspended on opposite sides of a blank silk-screened blue plexiglass panel.

**EXHIBITOR**
Penn Racquet Sports
**PRODUCER**
Cyclonics Inc., Medina, OH
**DESIGNERS**
Marty Spicuzza/Gina Roberson

The use of custom moldings, space frames, and a new color scheme gives this refurbished booth a new, contemporary look.

**EXHIBITOR**
Architectural Walls Ltd.
**PRODUCER**
Hartwig Exhibitions,
    Milwaukee, WI
**DESIGNER**
G.P. Lyons

The exhibitor's product is used
as part of the structure.

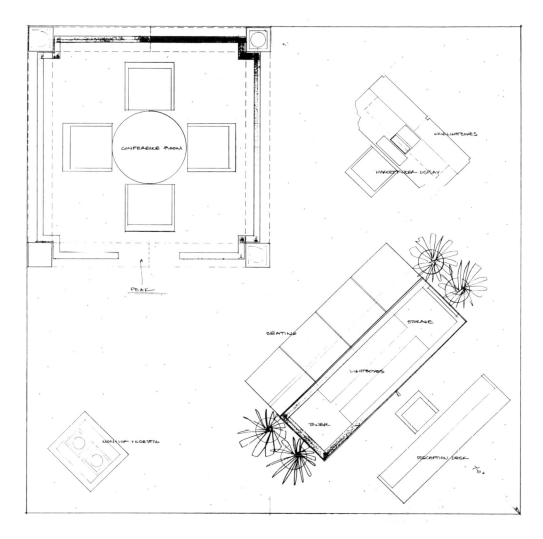

**EXHIBITOR**
Advo System Inc.
**PRODUCER**
John Oldham Studios Inc.,
  Wethersfield, CT
**DESIGNER**
Stephen Walsh

With only a 20'x20' island display, it was a challenge to include room for a conference area, a reception desk, storage, a video presentation, and a computer workstation. The problem was solved by establishing four independent areas that allowed clear sight lines and easy access into the booth. The tower, with its illuminated logo, was the backdrop for the reception desk. The open-frame conference room supported photographic appliques, and the computer workstation backed up to a modular light box.

**EXHIBITOR**
Pierce & Stevens Corp.
**PRODUCER**
Design for Industry Inc.,
    Buffalo, NY
**DESIGNERS**
Jack Snyder, Tim Dexter

To attract an audience interested in packaging materials, the back wall of this exhibit simulated a corrugated sheet ripped open to display a large photomural of packaging. The same material was used to wrap the three pedestals used for product display.

**EXHIBITOR**
Kitzing Inc.
**PRODUCER**
Kitzing Inc., Chicago, IL
**DESIGNER**
Fred Kitzing

The four panels with sales demonstration materials are supported solely by the overhead structure, leaving a maximum of floor area for selling in a 20' x 20' space.

**EXHIBITOR**
Pure Data
**PRODUCER**
J & O Exhibits, Toronto, ON
**DESIGNER**
Debbie Suddick

Four 16' towers with illuminated logos are connected by open mesh triangular grid panels. These define the space and give an open contemporary feeling. Eight information/demonstration stations at the bases of the tower permit individual demos of software.

**EXHIBITOR**
Duncan Aviation
**PRODUCER**
Bluepeter, San Francisco, CA
**DESIGNER**
Mitchell Mauk, Mauk Design,
    San Francisco, CA

Duncan Aviation, a jet
maintenance company, decided
to explain its leadership by
concentrating on its employees.
Consequently, it featured a series
of 19"x24" photographs of
people from each of its eight
major divisions. To include those
left out of the photos, every
employee signature was
reproduced in gold on the wing-
shaped central tower. The entire
structure was built on materials
directly from planes, or
resembling aviation parts.
Drilled-out stainless steel struts
supported white conference area
walls made of a new Japanese
plastic. Eight perforated steel
panels surrounded the portraits.
The translucency of this material
changes and it shows moires
depending on the viewer's
position. The green clips which
support the plex frames are
actually luggage tie-down hooks
from a Beechcraft, and an
aviation plunger-pin fastener
secures the black title bar to the
perforated steel.

**EXHIBITOR**
Evans & Sutherland
**PRODUCER**
Bluepeter, San Francisco, CA
**DESIGNER**
Mitchell Mauk, Mauk Design,
    San Francisco

This unusual booth featured a curved background, highlighted with alternating strips of polished and matte aluminum. Ports in each panel could be removed for computer cables to pass through, or for glass supports for computers and/or monitors. Custom-designed light fixtures could be adjusted and mounted to bring light where needed.

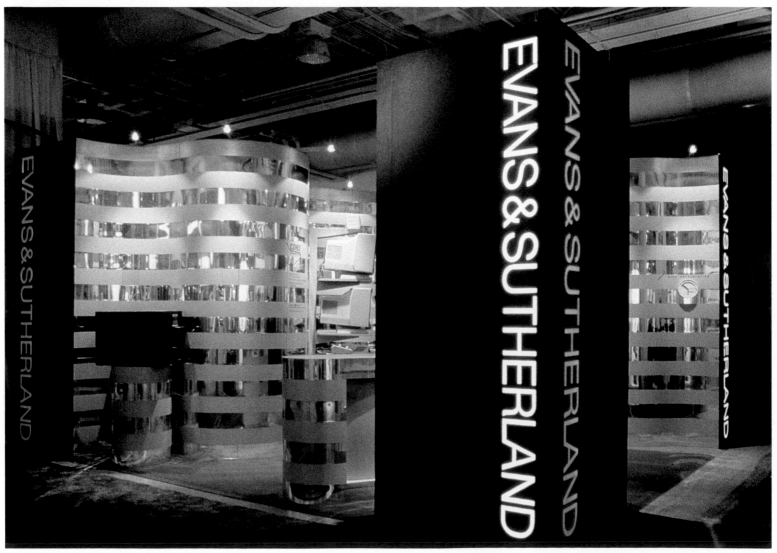

# CHAPTER
## 2

# MEDIUM
# EXHIBITS

**EXHIBITOR**
Relational Technology Inc.
**PRODUCER**
Bluepeter, San Francisco, CA
**DESIGNER**
Mitchell Mauk, Mauk Design,
San Francisco, CA

This exhibit was designed to show how one software product —Ingres—was serving many industries. It used industry-specific icons to convey the message, some enlarged and others reduced in scale. The exhibit's short set-up time allows easy adaptation to different trade shows, by adding or changing icons.

**EXHIBITOR**
Southwestern Bell Telephone
**PRODUCER**
Pingel Displays Inc., St. Louis, MO
**DESIGNER**
Wil Lutz

The open floor plan and strong graphics, with free-standing work stations, make this an inviting and functional exhibit. An in-line configuration is easily achieved.

**EXHIBITOR**
Avant Garde Optics
**PRODUCER**
United Longchamp Int'l.,
    Chicago, IL
**DESIGNER**
Baudouin Baltus

Constructed of a combination of Octanorm and Meroform, this exhibit had two entrances which portrayed a woman's face adorned with an oversized pair of sunglasses. White Formica display cases held 85 eyeglass frames.

**EXHIBITOR**
Marine Midland Automotive
  Finance Corp.
**PRODUCER**
Haas Display Co.,
  Minneapolis, MN
**DESIGNER**
Richard Giffin, Exhibit Design
  System

The basic material for this
exhibit was stone-textured, high-
pressure laminates. Routed
detailing simulated the seams
between stone blocks.

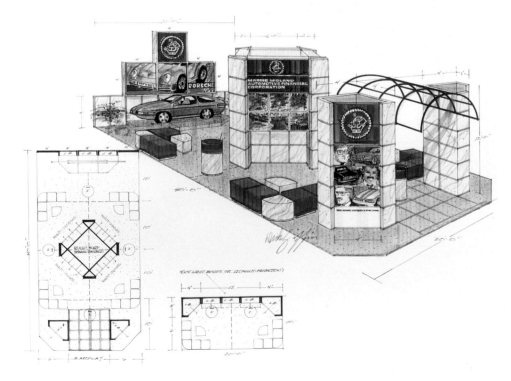

**EXHIBITOR**
Rofin Sinar
**PRODUCER**
Exhibitgroup San Francisco,
    So. San Francisco, CA
**DESIGNER**
Jayne Beetlestone

Although this exhibit looks like a custom design, it actually uses Octanorm elements. Note the protective wall that keeps visitors from approaching the demonstration units from the wrong side, without blocking their view.

**EXHIBITOR**
Beecham Labs
**PRODUCER**
Dimension Works Inc.,
    Bensenville, IL
**DESIGNER**
Stan Muklewicz

A combination of monolithic shapes and overhead structures provides Beecham Laboratories with a strong corporate image in the pharmaceutical industry. Easily interchangeable rear-illuminated signs and graphic panels permit versatility in product emphasis and booth configuration. It can be set up in 14', 12' and 8' heights.

**EXHIBITOR**
United Exposition Service;
    United Longchamp Int'l.
**PRODUCER**
United Longchamp International,
    Chicago, IL
**DESIGNER**
Baudouin Baltus

Outstanding is the extensive use of Drop Paper banners, suspended from a polished steel truss structure. The center lounge area, elevated on a platform, is illuminated from a hanging structure. Octanorm and Meroform elements are used throughout.

**EXHIBITOR**
Mannington Mills Inc.
**PRODUCER**
Exhibitgroup Atlanta, Atlanta, GA
**DESIGNER**
Mark S. Burns

Except for the reception area at one end of the 30' x 50' peninsula, the exhibit is completely enclosed. Distinctive treatment of product is created in recessed area, on the outside perimeter of the space as well as the interior, by collages of product taking on the aspect of art in a gallery.

**EXHIBITOR**
Emco Industries
**PRODUCER**
Herb Dixon & Assoc.,
    Des Moines, IA
**DESIGNER**
Herb Dixon

A mundane product, aluminum
storm doors, was given a high-
tech look, within a limited
budget, through the use of
Nimlok elements in a custom-
designed structure. An octagonal
structure, with storm doors on
six of its faces, was the center of
the display. Other elements
carried additional doors and
transparencies of the product.
The canopy, of clear plexiglass
and neon tubing, tied the unit
together. This, too, was made of
standard Nimlok panels and
connectors.

**EXHIBITOR**
Walt Disney Company
**PRODUCER**
Freeman Exhibit Co., Dallas, TX
**DESIGNER**
Jim Baridon

This exhibit, to promote many facets of the Disney operation, had room for 40 backlit Duratrans. The company name, on all four sides, was made with fiber optics, and the interior ceiling's blue glow could be brightened or darkened with a rheostat. Chaser lights on the inside of the headers added excitement.

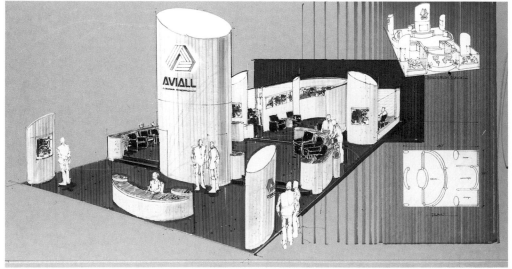

**EXHIBITOR**
Aviall
**PRODUCER**
Freeman Exhibit Co., Dallas, TX
**DESIGNERS**
Rudy Rich, Gary Artzt

The 20'-high elliptical tower is the centerpiece of this display. Finished in Zolatone, it contains a fiber optics display and carries a cutout metal logo. The elevated deck has custom seating and three entryways. There are two enclosed conference rooms which can be isolated with mini-blinds.

**EXHIBITOR**
Lucas Avitron
**PRODUCER**
Freeman Exhibit Co., Dallas, TX
**DESIGNER**
Gary Artzt

The curved 39″ walls are offset and attach to a cylinder containing fluorescent lights on both sides, creating a colored light wash on the walls. This arrangement also permits flexibility in the placing of the wall units. One-inch thick shelves of clear acrylic are recessed into the walls for the display of products.

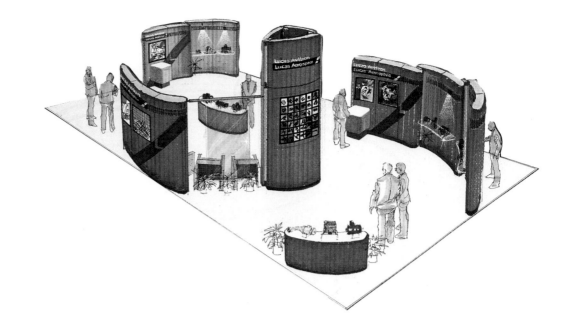

**EXHIBITOR**
Bauerfeind
**PRODUCER**
Exhibitgroup/Atlanta, Atlanta, GA
**DESIGNER**
Mark S. Burns

The exhibitor manufactures braces and supports for sports injuries, and wanted to feature three products. Each was given a pedestal near the aisles, facing the interior. This made it easy to qualify visitors at the aisle and register them at one of the two centrally-located literature/lead counters. The bulk of the display, including large, floating graphics, was kept high to produce strong recognition across the hall, leaving the underside open and airy. At the back of the space was a platform for live product demonstrations.

**EXHIBITOR**
ICI Baquacil
**PRODUCER**
Denby Associates, Princeton, NJ
**DESIGNER**
Tony Lualdi

To give visitors at this exhibit the feeling of being in a swimming pool, the streamlined modern shapes are painted with a white and blue flecked shape, and the carpet was designed to reflect the shapes of the units. Overhead heatwaves, in sun yellow and salmon, appear to warm the pool and complete the tropical ambience.

**EXHIBITOR**
**Magla Products**
**PRODUCER**
**Convention Exhibits Inc.,**
   **Chicago, IL**

This exhibit was intended to present products in a Victorian home. Parquet floors were used in part of the booth; an actual tin ceiling in a Victorian pattern, with recessed down lighting; Victorian-style tables and chairs. The slated roof has a patina copper finish.

**EXHIBITOR**
Serono Laboratories
**PRODUCER**
Davis Design Associates,
    Fitchburg, MA
**DESIGNER**
John M. Davis

Each of the free-standing
modules is devoted to an
individual fertility drug. The
center is a seating area for
informal and comfortable
discussions.

**EXHIBITOR**
**Denby Associates**
**PRODUCER**
**Denby Associates, Princeton, NJ**
**DESIGNER**
**Lisa Montgomery**

Light-washed overhead arches
and glossy white columns with
stepped gray bases establish
strong, sophisticated
architectural lines. All
components were built using a
sleeve-fit system that keeps set-
up time at a minimum.

77

**EXHIBITOR**
S&W
**PRODUCER**
Dimension Works Inc.,
    Bensenville, IL
**DESIGNER**
Bill Hofmockel

Traditional design combined
with modern materials and
finishes to allow this booth to
highlight a line of fine food
products. The rotating shelves in
the stand-alone cabinet called
attention to featured items, while
the entire line was displayed on
the back wall. Plexiglass with
etched logos fit into rails that
surrounded the semi-private
conference area on the left,
while Corian counters offered a
place on the right to taste
samples.

**EXHIBITOR**
Victoreen Inc.
**PRODUCER**
Communications Exhibits Inc.,
    Canal Fulton, OH
**DESIGNER**
David Jeffries

Two 50' structures, on opposite
sides of an aisle, control the
atmosphere. The extensive use
of oak and equipment alcoves
set Victoreen apart from more
flamboyant exhibitors.

**EXHIBITOR**
Thermador/Waste King
**PRODUCER**
Design South Inc., Atlanta, GA
**DESIGNER**
Joel Katzowitz

Units were displayed in kitchen-like settings, but with slanted counters to provide better viewing.

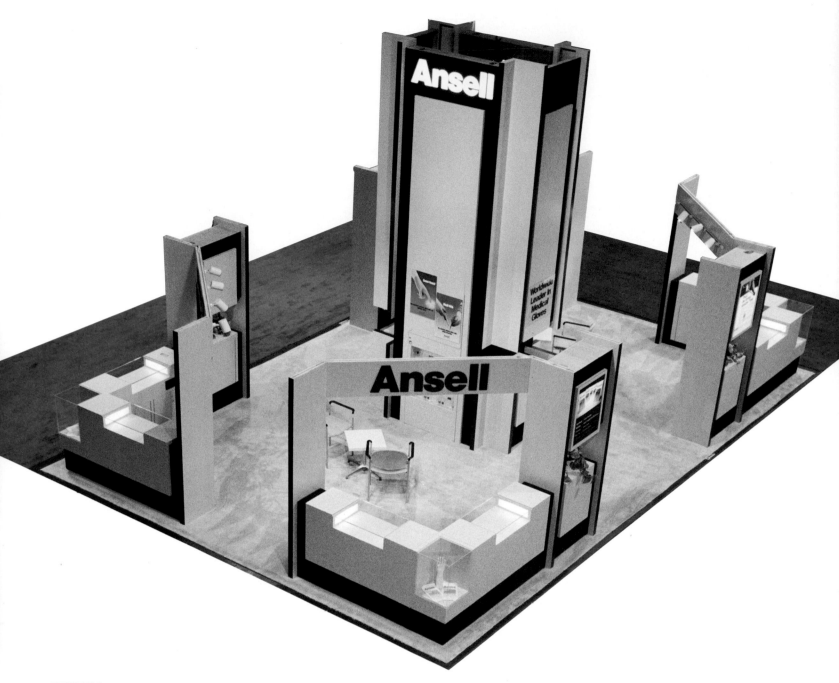

**EXHIBITOR**
**Ansell-Americas/Medical Division**
**PRODUCER**
**KMK Industries Inc.,**
    **Milwaukee, WI**
**DESIGNERS**
**Jack Wegner, Andy Hess**

Demonstration booths at all four
corners, plus a central tower, all
carry the company name for
rapid identification. The open
plan encourages traffic flow-
through.

**EXHIBITOR**
Artesian Industries
**PRODUCER**
Communication Exhibits Inc.,
    Canal Fulton, OH
**DESIGNER**
Brian Walters

The centerpiece of this exhibit is a 24' polished-chrome tambour column which supports four beams that feature the company name. Glass black laminate is used throughout to emphasize the product's delicate color. A glamour bathroom serves as a focal point in the center of the planned traffic flow.

**EXHIBITOR**
Video Treasures
**PRODUCER**
Communication Exhibits Inc.,
    Canal Fulton, OH
**DESIGNER**
Ernie Gotschall

The display pedestals hold 1/2''
thick vertical strips of plexi-glass,
on which product and photos
can be mounted with Velcro.
This permits easy rearrangement
of what is on display.

**EXHIBITOR**
Ferretti
**PRODUCER**
Kadoke Display Ltd.,
    Mississauga, ON
**DESIGNER**
Karen MacQuarrie

A truss structure, mounted on
the four corner units, supports a
four-sided identification sign.

**EXHIBITOR**
T-Fal Corporation
**PRODUCER**
KMK Industries, Milwaukee, WI
**DESIGNERS**
Jack Wegner, Andy Hess

Two separate divisions were combined in this exhibit to occupy an L-shaped space. A single corporate look with uninterrupted selling areas was achieved. Slotted backwall panels with glass shelves held product samples.

**EXHIBITOR**
Sidbec Dosco
**PRODUCER**
Les Concepts Polystand Inc.
**DESIGNERS**
Charles Godbout, Jean Fraser

The interlocked truss members, used throughout this exhibit, support and form the canopy, and hold back-lit transparencies. Note the use of a conveyor belt as a display table.

**EXHIBITOR**
Vestron Television
**PRODUCER**
1220 Exhibits Inc., Nashville, TN
**DESIGNER**
Claire O'Farrell

Illuminated light-boxes and neon tube identification look striking against high gloss black columns and headers. Human figures, also of high gloss black finish, serve as unusual pedestals for the light boxes.

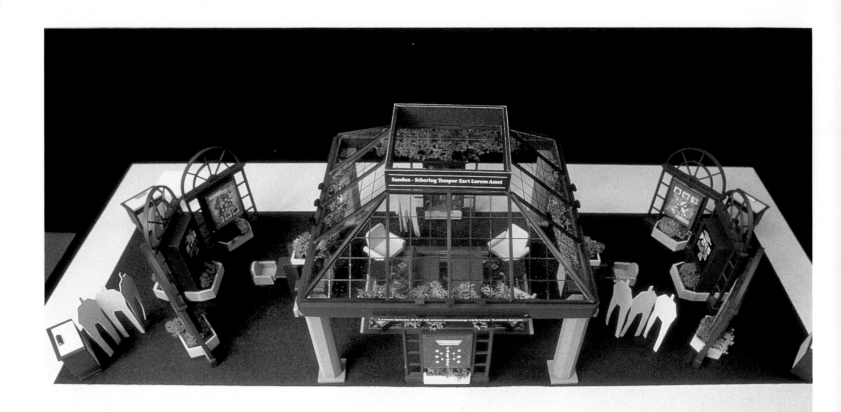

**EXHIBITOR**
Sandoz Pharmaceuticals/Schering-
   Plough
**PRODUCER**
Giltspur/Boston, Avon, MA
**DESIGNER**
John Barrett

A warm traditional environment,
using mahogany-stained
cabinetry and woodwork,
oriental rugs and leather chairs,
encouraged relaxation and
interaction. Six interactive
computer carrels provided
educational information on
current research in the field of
hematopoieses.

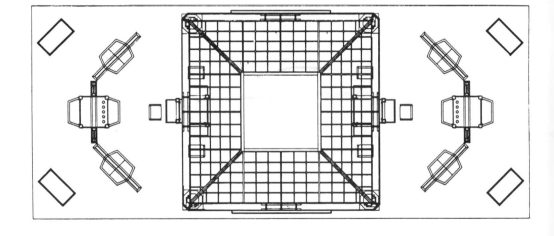

**EXHIBITOR**
Keller Tool
**PRODUCER**
Pingel Displays Inc., St. Louis, MO
**DESIGNER**
Wil Lutz

This island display offers high visibility for the actual product and for support graphics. It has easy hands-on capability, and two private conference rooms.

**EXHIBITOR**
Black & Decker
**PRODUCER**
Cyclonics Inc., Medina, OH
**DESIGNER**
Marty Spicuzza

Strong corporate and product identity was provided by large transparencies at the 14' high level. These created exceptional show floor visibility. Stained cedar was used to create an outdoor environment, while keeping within the corporate look desired by the exhibitor.

**EXHIBITOR**
Sandoz Pharmaceuticals;
    Allen and Hanburys
**PRODUCER**
Giltspur Exhibits/Boston;
    Avon, MA
**DESIGNER**
John Barrett

The organic shape of the heart muscle inspired the curving motif of the exhibit structure. Red neon traces an outline along the curves and contrasts sharply with the white walls. The finned ceiling structure provides an intimate atmosphere for seated work desks, which will evolve into interactive educational video stations at later installations.

**EXHIBITOR**
Metaugus
**PRODUCER**
United Longchamp Int'l.,
  Chicago, IL
**DESIGNER**
Babbe Lee

The tower, "floating" above a
black pyramid, successfully
caught the eye of show visitors.
The exhibit was constructed of
Exponent parts.

**EXHIBITOR**
**Chips**
**PRODUCER**
**Color & Design Exhibits Inc.,**
     **Portland, OR**

Double-sided demonstration
stations are set in three corners
of this island booth, with a
reception desk in the fourth. The
center holds a conference room,
screened off only by clear plastic
panel walls.

**EXHIBITOR**
Konover Associates
**PRODUCER**
John Oldham Studios,
    Wethersfield, CT
**DESIGNER**
Stephen Walsh

This exhibit used existing 10′ walls in a new configuration that included 9 conference rooms, a food island, and space for more than 50 site plans. Three 20′ identification towers supported an open frame truss with 3′ dimensional logo letters. The exterior header band unified the structure and formed the entrance archway.

CHAPTER

# 3

# LARGE
# EXHIBITS

**EXHIBITOR**
Lehndorff Property Management
**PRODUCER**
Kadoke Display Ltd.,
    Mississauga, ON
**DESIGNER**
Michael Klym

A company with a conservative reputation wanted to expand into high profile retail. Exciting graphics and modern structure contributed to this redefinition.

**EXHIBITOR**
Oneida
**PRODUCER**
Giltspur Exhibits/Rochester,
    Rochester, NY
**DESIGNER**
Jeanne Fornes

The repeated shapes, in two tones of gray, furnished an interesting background for the metal of the products on display.

**EXHIBITOR**
LaSalle Partners
**PRODUCER**
T.L. Horton Design Inc.,
    Dallas, TX
**DESIGNER**
Tony Horton

The theme of this exhibit was taken from the exhibitor's corporate offices in Chicago. The corner entrance to the exhibit was 25' high and 5' deep, evoking a typical Chicago urban office building entry. The arches and tile flooring continued this look. Zolatone was sprayed on scored wood panels to simulate pre-cast stone.

**EXHIBITOR**
NEC America
**PRODUCER**
Kitzing Inc., Chicago, IL
**DESIGNER**
James Hanlon

Hands-on product areas and broadcast quality settings demonstrate the exhibitor's state-of-the-art systems in a high-tech setting.

**EXHIBITOR**
Kangaroos USA
**PRODUCER**
Freeman Exhibit Co., Dallas, TX
**DESIGNER**
Tom Yurkin

Each corner of this simulated wrestling ring held a display case whose outside wall of reflective material was surrounded by vertical fluorescent tubes. Strobe lighting added excitement, as did two fog machines and a PA system. The central structure housed a conference room.

**EXHIBITOR**
Kaltenbach & Voigt & Co.
**PRODUCER**
Fairconsult GmbH, Köln,
  Germany
**DESIGNER**
Ludwig Ense

An unusual perimeter shape adds interest to this booth, in which dental equipment is displayed. The circular motif of the central raised platform is repeated in the two structures supported on columns on either side.

**EXHIBITOR**
Burger King Corporation
**PRODUCER**
T.L. Horton Design Inc.,
    Dallas, TX
**DESIGNER**
Tony Horton

A neutral background of gray
zolotone covered the walls of
the custom-red, metal grid
tower—a vibrant focal point for
the exhibit. Logo signage on
both sides of the 25'-foot high
tower was spot-lit from above
and back-lit within the tower. A
halo-lit map of the United States
featured regional offices, and
visuals on the walls showed
examples of restaurants
throughout the country.

**EXHIBITOR**
Oshkosh Truck
**PRODUCER**
Hartwig Exhibitions,
    Milwaukee, WI
**DESIGNER**
G.P. Lyons

With actual equipment big
enough to dominate the space,
all that was needed was
attractive units to identify the
exhibitor and demarcate the
space.

**EXHIBITOR**
Borden Foods
**PRODUCER**
Dimension Works, Bensenville, IL
**DESIGNER**
Tom Schowalter

This island booth, 40' x 85',
features six stair-stepped product
display modules with glass
shelves for product. At each end
of the booth, an overhead
archway rests on two of these
modules. The center structure
incorporates storage and two
conference rooms. Gloss
laminates are used throughout to
project a clean dairy
environment.

101

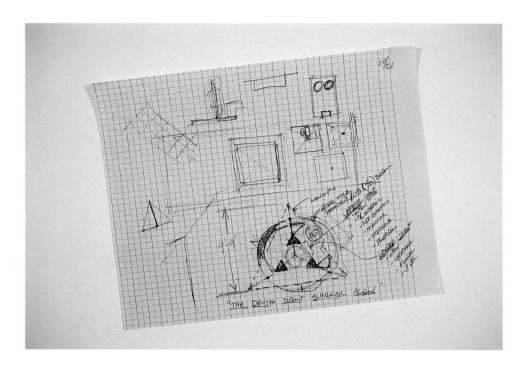

**EXHIBITOR**
Medtronic
**PRODUCER**
Design South Inc., Atlanta, GA
**DESIGNERS**
Scott Saunders, Gary Stewart

The use of custom-fabricated aluminum components allows great flexibility in configuration. Lighting fixtures on the canopy shine up and are colored with gels, so that each product area can be given its own identity. The gels, mounted by hook, loop for flexibility. Large product transparencies are displayed without copy.

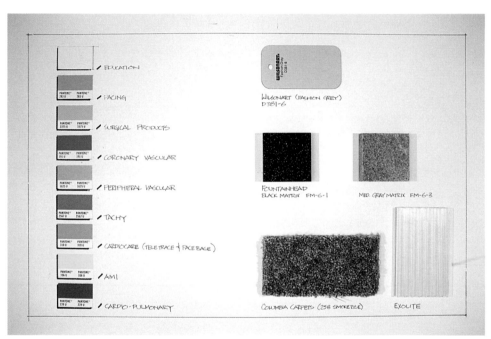

**EXHIBITOR**
Bell & Howell
**PRODUCER**
Exhibit by Design,
    Arlington Heights, IL
**DESIGNER**
Jeffrey Burke

This exhibit is 14' high, with 10'
clearance under the large
headers. The theater seats 24
people and can hold a standing
audience of 100. After each
presentation, the audience is
directed into two individual
office settings for personal
demonstrations. A 300 square-
foot upper deck holds
conference rooms, and creates a
much needed storage room
below.

**EXHIBITOR**
Westwood
**PRODUCER**
Design for Industry, Buffalo, NY
**DESIGNERS**
Jack Snyder, Andrea Billias,
   Tim Dexter, Tamara Dowd,
   Greg Meadows

This started as a 20'x80' exhibit and was expanded after one year to a 40'x50', across-the-aisle configuration. A central conference area was surrounded by individual product spaces, each with a demonstration table. The truss structure was not only decorative, but also unified the total space.

**EXHIBITOR**
ConAgra
**PRODUCER**
Exhibitgroup Atlanta, Atlanta, GA
**DESIGNER**
Michael Edwards

Many brands had to be unified by an umbrella structure, while allowing each to have its own focus point and demonstration area. The center enclosed a kitchen that supplied product for sampling of each section.

**EXHIBITOR**
Alside
**PRODUCER**
Cyclonics Inc., Medina, OH
**DESIGNERS**
Marty Spicuzza, Gina Roberson

The architectural design reflects the nature of the product. Canopies, lit from below, add a colorful element.

**EXHIBITOR**
Snapper Lawnmower
**PRODUCER**
1220 Exhibits Inc., Nashville, TN
**DESIGNER**
Miriam Owen

To reflect their Southern roots and friendly neighborhood store marketing, the designer used a white-columned display with a cedar shake roof as the centerpiece of the 40'x65' booth. There was ample room for the display of large equipment, as well as an interior area for portable products and accessories.

**EXHIBITOR**
Konami
**PRODUCER**
Dimension Works, Bensenville, IL
**DESIGNER**
Susan Kemble

The main entrance to this booth was an archway with sides made of graduated towers leading up to the company name. This structure was repeated on the opposite corner, but that arch led to a raised platform which held conference rooms.

**EXHIBITOR**
Amoco Performance Products
**PRODUCER**
Cyclonics Inc., Medina, OH
**DESIGNER**
Martin Spicuzza

This exhibit consists of a series of 5 modules mounted on casters for ease of set-up and flexibility in space adaptations. Since the exhibitor uses only island spaces, all modules are double-sided. The panels are attached with threaded aluminum stand-offs. Product samples mount on laminate panels applied to the slanted shelf with Velcro. The modules are connected by arched trusses which hold logo lightboxes. A 25' high tower gives excellent corporate identification.

**EXHIBITOR**
Miller Fluid Power
**PRODUCER**
Kitzing Inc., Chicago, IL
**DESIGNER**
James Hanlon

This open design, with its quiet presence, states the exhibitor's leadership in its field. Selling and demonstration stations are scattered around the periphery, while the central unit includes two conference rooms.

**EXHIBITOR**
Sterling Plumbing Group
**PRODUCER**
Convention Exhibits Inc.,
    Chicago, IL
**DESIGNERS**
Matthew Wycislak, John Keller

The column and post system
permits many booth
configurations with varied aisles
and traffic lanes. It also offers an
opportunity to dramatically show
products as they would appear
in a kitchen or bath setting.

**EXHIBITOR**
Westwood
**PRODUCER**
Design for Industry, Buffalo, NY
**DESIGNER**
Jack Snyder, Andrea Billias,
   Tim Dexter, Tamara Dowd,
   Greg Meadows

This started as a 20′ x 80′ exhibit and was expanded after one year to a 40′ x 50′, across-the-aisle configuration. A central conference area was surrounded by individual product spaces, each with a demonstration table. The truss structure was not only decorative, but also unified the total space.

**EXHIBITOR**
Hartmann Luggage
**PRODUCER**
1220 Exhibits Inc., Nashville, TN
**DESIGNER**
Claire O'Farrell

Subtle color changes and geometric display pods drew the eye to the luggage. Three conference rooms were built into this display, which simulated a retail store.

**EXHIBITOR**
Government of Singapore
**PRODUCER**
Kadoke Display Ltd.,
    Mississauga, ON
**DESIGNER**
Kingsmen Designers & Producers
    Pte Ltd., Signapore

This cross-aisle exhibit used interior-lit vacuum-formed motif panels.

**EXHIBITOR**
Diebold
**PRODUCER**
Communication Exhibits Inc.,
    Canal Fulton, OH
**DESIGNER**
Brian Walters

This modular exhibit can be
used in every configuration from
50′ x 50′ to in-line exhibits as
small as 10′. The height can also
be varied to meet show rules.

# CHAPTER

# 4

# GIANT EXHIBITS

**EXHIBITOR**
DuPont/Electronics
**PRODUCER**
Dimensional Studios Inc.,
    Runnemede, NJ
**DESIGNER**
John M. Sereduke

The product story is told primarily through back-lit transparencies, mounted in modular units. The largest configuration is 50′x115′, and promotes approximately 32 different product groups. The middle-sized exhibit is 20′x80′, and is actually three peninsulas with the header crossing two aisles. The third photo shows the use of a section to create a 10′x20′ configuration.

**EXHIBITOR**
The Cafaro Co.
**PRODUCER**
Greyhound Exposition Services,
  Las Vegas, NV
**DESIGNER**
Shelton Adell

The main entrance of this space, approximately 72' x 133', uses marble flooring, brass columns, plant holders, and cut-out letters to give a strong impression of solidity. The space, almost entirely closed around the perimeter, includes 20 private conference rooms, three executive offices, and a large hospitality area.

**EXHIBITOR**
Pontiac Motor Div.,
    General Motors
**PRODUCER**
Rowe Thomas Display Co.,
    Plymouth, MI
**DESIGNER**
Stuart Stone

This display was the centerpiece
of the total Pontiac exhibit. The
concept vehicle was placed on a
turntable, while a video show
interacted with a narrator.
Lighting and sound were
incorporated into the
presentation.

The open feeling of this exhibit invites the passer-by to step in. The two ''cars'' allow designers to view items in their approximate position for easier recognition. The four units shown in the Electrical/Electronic Systems section were used alone in a 30' configuration at another show.

**EXHIBITOR**
Navistar International
**PRODUCER**
Displaycraft Inc., Rockford, IL
**DESIGNER**
Corey Adelman

The new products being introduced at this show—massive tractors—were the stars of the exhibit, mounted on lit elevated platforms. The design project included developing the graphics on the trucks.

**EXHIBITOR**
**GMC Truck Division**
**PRODUCER**
**Exhibitgroup Chicago, Elk Grove**
    **Village, IL**
**DESIGNER**
**Rick Lewis**

Designed to show the high-tech image that trucks have achieved in recent years, this exhibit uses polished metal and special light fixtures to display its vehicles.

**EXHIBITOR**
Masco Corporation
**PRODUCER**
Kitzing Inc., Chicago, IL
**DESIGNERS**
Fred Kitzing, James Hanlon

The exhibits of 14 Masco companies were brought together under a corporate tower and beam structure. The 180' x 150' consolidated exhibit was the largest in the history of the National Association of Home Builders show.

**EXHIBITOR**
Cessna
**PRODUCER**
The Design Centre, Wichita, KS
**DESIGNER**
Curtis Harshfield

The 60'x60' space was created as a showcase for the exhibitor's Citation III. The curving platform in the rear, made of glass blocks, used sequential lighting to attract visitors towards the airplane mock-up. A 60'x10' space across the aisle featured two sales offices, customer information center, and a large storage room.

**EXHIBITOR**
Viacom Enterprises
**PRODUCER**
The Design Center, Wichita, KS
**DESIGNER**
Curtis Harshfield

Clustering of offices yields maximum space efficiency, while allowing for two large conference rooms, four offices, 16 screening rooms, a staff workbreak area, a raised stage, a bar, and three lobby seating areas, in a 7,000 square-foot area.

**EXHIBITOR**
Dynatech
**PRODUCER**
Color & Design Exhibits Inc.,
    Portland, OR

The reception area was placed
in one corner of this large island
space, with strong identification
facing in all four directions.
Viewing booths, placed on the
periphery, helped direct traffic.

**EXHIBITOR**
Fujitsu Inc. of America
**PRODUCER**
Rave Reviews, Mesa, AZ
**DESIGNER**
Tom Cameron

The circular pipe structure suggests the worldwide nature of the exhibitor. It is shown here in a 60'x70' space, but can also break down to a 40'x40' configuration without losing its full circle. It includes a stage area, two conference rooms and a reception area.

**EXHIBITOR**
Oneida
**PRODUCER**
Giltspur Exhibits/Rochester,
    Rochester, NY
**DESIGNER**
Jeanne Fornes

The repeated shapes, in two tones of gray, furnished an interesting background for the metal of the products on display.

**EXHIBITOR**
Magicsilk
**PRODUCER**
Exhibitgroup Atlanta, Atlanta, GA

Under a canopy of truss work spanning an 80′x60′ area, the various product lines are separated into shops and boutiques. An 8′ diameter globe represents the theme ''The World of Magicsilk,'' the largest manufacturer and importer of silk plants and flowers.

# CHAPTER
# 5
# MULTI-LEVEL EXHIBITS

**EXHIBITOR**
Hitachi
**PRODUCER**
Giltspur Exhibits/Rochester,
    Rochester, NY
**DESIGNER**
Ray Crouch

A system using both opaque and smoked plastic panels is used to form massive columns and an upper level with conference areas. Company identification is outstanding, and equipment is demonstrated on the ground floor.

**EXHIBITOR**
Equity Properties &
    Development Co.
**PRODUCER**
T.L. Horton Design Inc.,
    Dallas, TX
**DESIGNER**
Tony Horton

This exhibit is designed to reflect the playful, festive approach the exhibitor takes in its retail development projects. The back portion of the peninsular exhibit has a second level. Letters, 8' high and 12'' deep, are backed by a 10' high, 40' long red banner, stretched on a metal frame, to give exceptional visibility. Free standing, double-sided display units, 10' 6'' high, hold transparencies showing shopping center projects. These units could be used in smaller conventions and free-standing in center openings. Clusters of balloons conceal the structural column in the exhibit space.

**EXHIBITOR**
Amoco Chemical Co.
**PRODUCER**
Cyclonics Inc., Medina, OH
**DESIGNERS**
Martin Spicuzza, Gina Roberson

This exhibit marked the entry of Amoco as a full-time plastics supplier. A fast-paced video-wall presentation, at one corner of the booth, told the unified story of the newly-expanded company. Individual products were incorporated on the main level, each in its own selling space. Many Amoco products were included in the structure, including the overhead lattice of beams. The fabric used on the floor, the walls, and the furniture was from another division. The two conference areas, nestled among the truss structure, were reached via a central staircase.

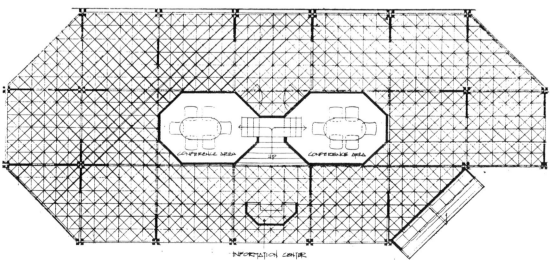

**EXHIBITOR**
L.J. Hooker Developments
**PRODUCER**
T.L. Horton Design Inc.,
    Dallas, TX
**DESIGNER**
Tony Horton

With entertainment as the theme, and carousels as its symbol, this exhibit has a 27' domed entry. A color scheme of salmon and white, with a turquoise accent, complements the laminated marble floor and granite-like Zolatone walls. A "fifties" style deli, created to serve food, has a custom bar, and black and white laminated tile floor. Backlit transparency boxes, as large as 4'x8', feature projects. Its two levels offer 28 custom offices with glass walls. The exhibit has its own air handling system for the deck and office areas.

**EXHIBITOR**
NEC
**PRODUCER**
Kadoke Display Ltd.,
   Mississauga, ON
**DESIGNER**
John Teager

This exhibit maximized display
space in a limited area. A truss,
supported by narrow columns,
unified and outlined the space.

**EXHIBITOR**
Zenith Data Systems
**PRODUCER**
Exhibit by Design,
    Arlington Heights, IL
**DESIGNER**
Jeffrey Burke

This 70' x 70' exhibit can be configured for smaller spaces. Its most interesting feature is security for the computers on display. They are lowered electronically into their pedestals, then a lockable lid drops down. The product on larger counters is protected with steel roll-down electric doors. The upper deck, while visually open, contains four totally private conference rooms, a reception desk and lobby area. All the vertical blue stripes are rear illuminated to create an eye-catching look.

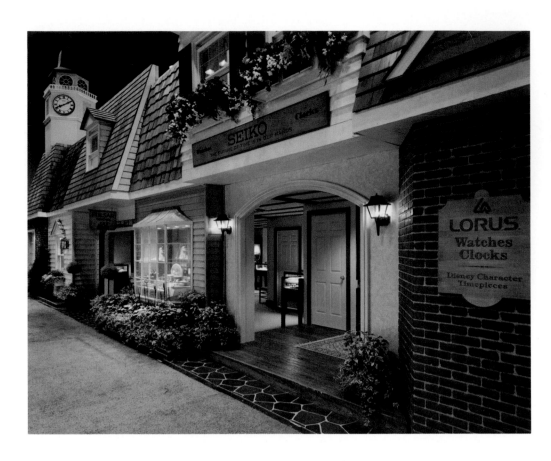

**EXHIBITOR**
Hattori Corporation
**PRODUCER**
Lynch Exhibits, Pennsauken, NJ
**DESIGNER**
Don Reckeweg

Four watch companies, all subsidiaries of Hattori, combined to produce this village of shops and store windows. On the second level, behind the steep shingled roof, were conference rooms and a refreshment area.

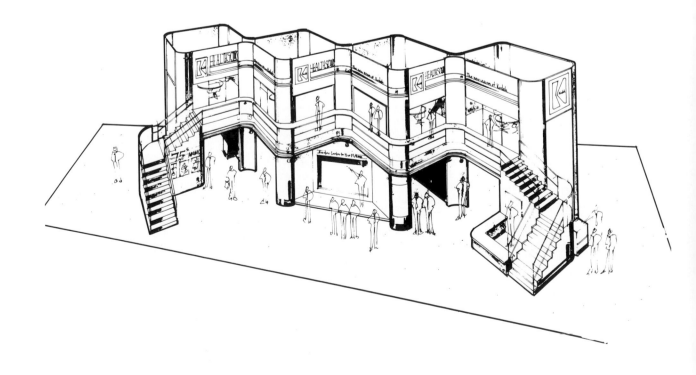

**EXHIBITOR**
Kodak Health Sciences
**PRODUCER**
John Oldham Studios,
    Wethersfield, CT
**DESIGNERS**
Stephen Walsh, Stephen Perez

Four upper-level conference
rooms were reached by an
outside walk-way that connected
stairs at both ends. Product
display bays and light boxes
were under the conference
rooms and headers extended
from the central structure.
Lightweight, short beams
avoided the necessity for rigging
labor, and the design permitted
all electrical work to be done
after assembly, eliminating labor
overlap.

**EXHIBITOR**
MMS International
**PRODUCER**
Cyclonics Inc., Medina, OH
**DESIGNERS**
Marty Spicuzza, Gina Roberson,
   Anthony Santarelli

This booth provides exceptional
impact for such small space. The
upper level contains a simulated
control area which demonstrates
the computer control system in a
factory situation.

**EXHIBITOR**
EZ Paintr Corp.
**PRODUCER**
KMK Industries, Inc.
 Milwaukee, WI
**DESIGNER**
Jack Wegner

There are five conference rooms on the second level, and two private conference/presentation rooms on the first level. The latter rooms feature rear projection for slides and videotapes, and display windows that change from translucent white to clear, at the touch of a button, for dramatic product presentation. Strong brand identity is accomplished with 50' lighted headers on each side of the booth. The feature area at one end, for live presentations and demos, has a floor-to-ceiling rear projection screen.

**EXHIBITOR**
Hewlett-Packard
**PRODUCER**
Newton Display Group Ltd.,
    Manchester, UK
**DESIGNER**
Furneaux Stewart

Telecom, held in Geneva every four years, is where multinational companies compete to convey their technological innovations in all the fields in which they participate. Show management was persuaded to double the allowable height, permitting a three tier structure, with an increase of space from 350 to 854 square meters. The unusual shape created a dramatic impact on visitors, and the people mover carried visitors rapidly through a series of sophisticated audio-visual messages, backed up with video and live presentations.

**EXHIBITOR**
Honeywell/Residential
**PRODUCER**
Haas Display Co.,
    Minneapolis, MN
**DESIGNER**
Richard Giffin, Exhibit Design
Systems

A 10-foot-square, upper level conference area is surrounded by three product display panels, each surmounted by a large, double-faced transparency holder.

**EXHIBITOR**
Toshiba ISD
**PRODUCER**
Kadoke Display Ltd.,
   Mississauga, ON
**DESIGNERS**
Vio Manga, Jaqueline Crawley,
John Teager

Originally, this exhibit was built around a central theater area, topped with company signage. Two years later, in 1989, when more room was needed, a lounge area was built above the theater, using Octonorm elements. Newly designed showcases and ground floor offices were also added.

**EXHIBITOR**
Singapore Tourist Promotion
    Board
**PRODUCER**
Pico Art International Pte Ltd.,
    Singapore

Developed for the world's fair in
Brisbane, Australia, the central
theme was "Surprising
Singapore." A miniature street
scene was comprised of
traditional Chinese, Indian and
Malay quarters. Colorful displays,
graphics and descriptions helped
draw visitors through the entire
multi-level exhibit.

**EXHIBITOR**
Hobart Inc.
**PRODUCER**
Dimension Works Inc.,
  Bensenville, IL
**DESIGNER**
Stan Muklewicz

The center has three conference rooms on two upper deck levels, with a gallery of product displays and transparencies below. Cantilevered aluminum trusses suspend lighting fixtures over the large pieces of equipment displayed by the aisles.

**EXHIBITOR**
Singapore Defence Industries
**PRODUCER**
Pico Art International Pte Ltd.,
  Singapore
**DESIGNERS**
Derek Corke, Cheng Eng Kek

This is designed to blend with the high-flying image of an aerospace show. Its impressive double decks, tall lighted neon towers and pillars, and clever manipulation of graphics, helped to enhance the entire image of the booth.

**EXHIBITOR**
Husky Injection Molding Systems
**PRODUCER**
Kitzing Inc., Chicago, IL
**DESIGNER**
Joe Panzarella

The conference balcony was positioned to overlook a massive new piece of operating machinery which could also be inspected from ground level.

**EXHIBITOR**
Cooper Rolls
**PRODUCER**
Communication Exhibits Inc.,
    Canal Fulton, OH
**DESIGNER**
Brian Walters

The size of a complete gas
turbine unit was emphasized
with a three-dimensional
structure based on a CAD
blueprint rendition. The air
intake unit, on the left, housed a
conference room.

**EXHIBITOR**
Code-A-Phone
**PRODUCER**
Lewellen & Best, Montgomery, IL
**DESIGNER**
Paul Stahlberg

The center of the exhibit is an unusual truncated pyramid shape that contains conference areas on its second floor. The shape is repeated for free-standing units, and inverted for counters.

**EXHIBITOR**
Raymond Weil
**PRODUCER**
KPW Productions, New York
**DESIGNER**
Pichai

This discreet design has display
windows built into the columns
that support an upper level and
a canvas canopy. Showing
expensive watches, most of the
space for talking and showing is
not fully visible from the aisles.

**EXHIBITOR**
Quaker Food Service
**PRODUCER**
Dimension Works, Bensenville, IL
**DESIGNER**
Susan Kemble

Each of the four arms of the structure shows the products of a different division of the company, while the central unit shows menus comprising products from the four divisions. The two-story structure in the rear contains a full kitchen on the ground level, where sample menus are prepared and presented at tables between these two units. There are three conference rooms on the second level. The familiar Quaker Oats box rotates to form an attractive booth identification.

**EXHIBITOR**
Dupli-Color Products Co.
**PRODUCER**
Kitzing Inc., Chicago, IL
**DESIGNER**
Cynthia Dunaj

Giant reproductions of aerosol cans called attention to a new product and served as supports for a second story conference center. The exhibit highlighted new point-of-purchase units for a product just being introduced to the automotive industry.

**EXHIBITOR**
Champion Products Inc.
**PRODUCER**
Ontario Design, Rochester, NY
**DESIGNER**
Thomas Finn

Summer in the Park was the theme of this open booth. The park was peopled with 10 models wearing various athletic garments. The video wall showed a retrospective on product enhancements and the current advertising and merchandising programs. The second story had two general conference areas, plus additional selling stations. Extensive use of click panels, custom panels, and extrusions with metal grid systems provided attractive environments.

CHAPTER

# 6

## SPECIAL AREAS

**EXHIBITOR**
Singer Sewing Machine Co.
**PRODUCER**
1220 Exhibits Inc., Nashville, TN
**DESIGNER**
Miriam Owen

The eye-catcher in this exhibit was a 12' replica of a sewing machine head, which served to identify the exhibitor and draw traffic into the booth. Most of the booth area was devoted to working machines being demonstrated. In the rear of the exhibit, partially cut off by the information desk, was a comfortable lounging area where refreshments were served. Private conference rooms led off this area.

**EXHIBITOR**
Mead Johnson Pharmaceuticals
**PRODUCER**
Giltspur Exhibits/Boston,
 Avon, MA
**DESIGNER**
John Barrett

To promote an anti-anxiety drug geared to the elderly, the exhibitor concentrated on the classic symptoms of anxiety. Larger-than-life photographs, in black and white, portrayed elderly people with expressions typical of anxiety. This theme was supplemented by ''live sculptures,'' mimes who depicted expressions of anxiety. This became the exhibit's stopping and holding power. To avoid competing with the photos and the actors, structures of Alusett extrusions served as both stage and gallery wall.

**EXHIBITOR**
Honeywell/Building Controls Div.
**PRODUCER**
Haas Display Co.,
    Minneapolis, MN
**DESIGNER**
Richard Giffin

The sixteen screen videowall played a pre-recorded video presentation when it was not being used as part of an interactive show with a live presenter and an electronically-generated character. Hands-on product demonstrations were given throughout the large booth.

**EXHIBITOR**
**Legend Sporting Goods**
**PRODUCER**
**Technical Exhibits Corp.**
**DESIGNER**
**David Giambrone, GAMS,**
   **Chicago, IL**

This simple exhibit, made with
TechExhibit portable and
modular exhibit system, permits
the visitor to try the product.

**EXHIBITOR**
Jacobs Suchard Canada
**PRODUCER**
Advanced Exhibit Methods,
    Santa Ana, CA
**DESIGNER**
A.M. Han

This exhibit utilizes Futura
System 1 elements, and includes
a kitchen with sink and drain
facilities, where coffee can be
roasted, ground, brewed and
served.

**EXHIBITOR**
Simitar Entertainment Inc.
**PRODUCER**
Haas Display Co.,
    Minneapolis, MN
**DESIGNER**
Richard Giffin

This open booth, designed as an idealized video store, has 10 player/monitor stations to encourage browsing and demonstration of videotapes. All titles are mounted on slatwall to encourage their use.

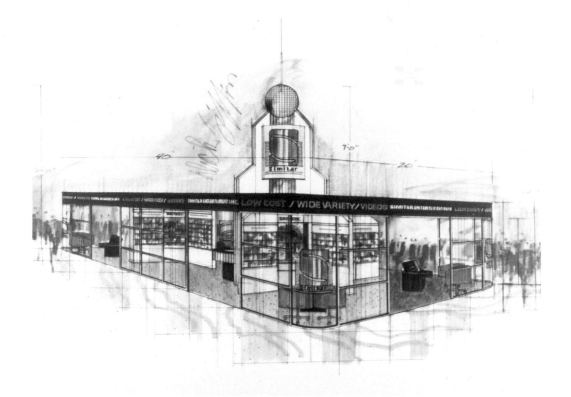

**EXHIBITOR**
Valmet Paper Machinery
**PRODUCER**
The Display Shop Inc., Dale, WI
**DESIGNER**
Joanne Carlson

This exhibit features a computer-controlled light show at one end of the space, where raised silver letters are illuminated from behind. The lighting varies in color and brilliance in harmony with recordings of Sibelius' music, chosen to reflect the exhibitor's Finnish origin. The furniture throughout the booth was custom built, using vinyl coverings with laminate tops. Literature was housed in wedge-shaped laminate units, and vinyl banners were used for signage. The post and beam construction held track lighting, with all wiring inside the beams.

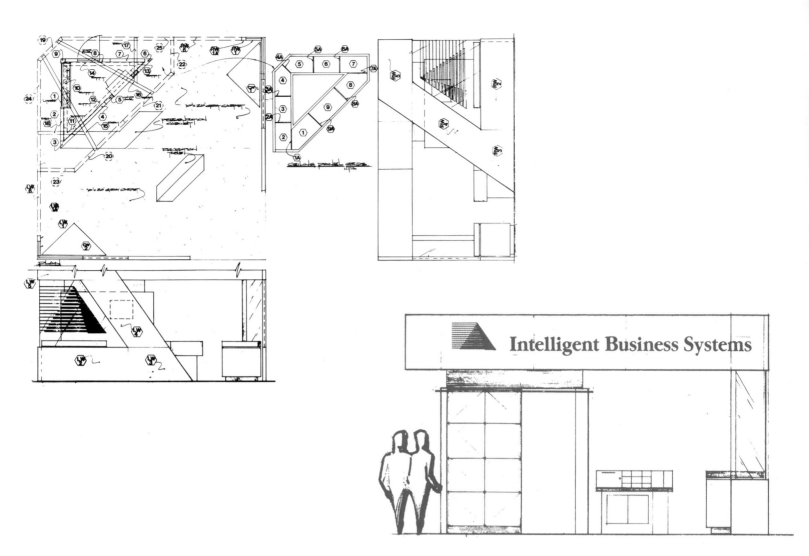

Intelligent Business Systems

Intelligent Business Systems

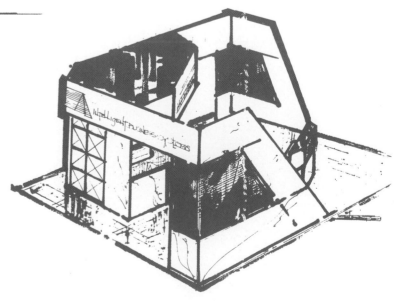

**EXHIBITOR**
Intelligent Business Systems
**PRODUCER**
John Oldham Studios,
    Wethersfield, CT
**DESIGNER**
James L. Colbert

To introduce a new computer program in a 20' x 20' booth, a triangular presentation area was developed for one corner of the space. The backwall supported a 27" monitor, and included space for the mainframe computer and related equipment. The presentation cabinet had a shelf for the keyboard and a small monitor, allowing the demonstrator to keep an eye on the screen while facing his audience. A cantilevered header helps to subdue ambient lighting that falls on the monitor. Smaller demonstration stations are located at the wings of the large structure, and a centrally located reception counter faces the entrance to the booth.

**EXHIBITOR**
Wang
**PRODUCER**
Chicago Scenic Studios, Live
    Marketing, (both) Chicago, IL
**DESIGNER**
Linda Buchanan, R.D. Design
    Assoc., Chicago

A live presentation explained the capabilities of Wang Integrated Imaging Systems. In a closed-environment presentation, the first sequence used a miniature office building with light box windows to explain the problems of a company called "Typico." Later rooms showed solutions at various levels of sophistication.

**EXHIBITOR**
Mitsubishi
**PRODUCER**
United Longchamps Int'l,
    Chicago, IL
**DESIGNER**
Baudouin Baldus

Seating in the theater area was constructed from Meroform elements. Drop Paper banners with the company name were used for the backwall of the stage. The dome over the reception desk included the company's three-diamond logo.

**EXHIBITOR**
**Teradyne Connection Systems**
**PRODUCER**
**Fahey Exhibits, Northboro, MA**
**DESIGNER**
**Robert Segal, Segal Design,**
   **Arlington, MA**

This display, designed to attract visitors from a distance, gave a dynamic explanation of the advantages of the exhibitor's electronic connectors. By separating the control panel from the main display structure, visitors were kept at the optimum viewing distance. A solid-state electronic display, keyed with light boxes, created the moving images. These ran constantly until the visitor manually interrupted the cycle to explore information specific to his needs.

**EXHIBITOR**
Hewlett-Packard
**PRODUCER**
Davis Design Associates,
   Fitchburg, MA
**DESIGNER**
John M. Davis

The two-story tower serves as a backdrop for regularly scheduled live demonstrations. The truss system extending from the wall helps protect the screens from ambient light.

**EXHIBITOR**
Crane/National Vendors
**PRODUCER**
Pingel Displays Inc.
**DESIGNERS**
Bob Meyer/Bill Wilson

Almost the entire wall of this 20′ x 120′ in-line exhibit held banks of vending machines, unified with a bubble canopy and marble fascia. A performance area was placed in the center of the unit, and a hospitality area was located at one end.

**EXHIBITOR**
**Honeywell Residential Controls**
**PRODUCER**
**Haas Display Co.,**
**Minneapolis, MN**
**DESIGNER**
**Richard Giffin**

While this exhibit was essentially picked up from the structure developed for the previous year's show, a small presentation stage, with room for an audience of a dozen, was incorporated for a live performance by Live Marketing, Inc.

**EXHIBITOR**
Dainippon Screen
**PRODUCER**
Dimension Works Inc.,
    Bensenville, IL
**DESIGNER**
Freedom Design Group, Japan

Dominating this 150' x 60' space is a central theater structure which carries the exhibitor identification. It has a climate controlled computer equipment room and a private viewing area for live demonstrations. Each tier of the theater building is illuminated by a wash of halogen lighting from below.

**EXHIBITOR**
Anacomp
**PRODUCER**
Exhibit by Design, Arlington
   Heights, IL
**DESIGNER**
Jeffrey Burke

An enclosed video wall theater,
seating 50 people, is located in
the center of the exhibit. Its two
exits lead people directly into
one of the two product areas,
depending on their interest.

**EXHIBITOR**
Duracell USA
**PRODUCER**
Hartwig Exhibitions,
   Milwaukee, WI
**DESIGNER**
G.P. Lyons

The 15-screen videowall attracts passers-by, but the real attraction is furnished by the multiple demonstration stations on high counters, where visitors can use the exhibitor's new tester with a minimum of assistance.

**EXHIBITOR**
VPI
**PRODUCER**
Hartwig Exhibitions,
   Milwaukee, WI
**DESIGNER**
G.P. Lyons

This simple exhibit demonstrates the product at floor of the booth.

**EXHIBITOR**
Hamilton Beach
**PRODUCER**
Hartwig Exhibitions,
    Milwaukee, WI
**DESIGNER**
G.P. Lyons

This compact exhibit displays products and packaging in cabinets, and places its conference rooms on the upper level. Two demonstration booths face two aisles, where appliances can be demonstrated in use.

**EXHIBITOR**
Beecham-Upjohn
**PRODUCER**
Dimension Works, Bensenville, IL
**DESIGNER**
Stan Muklewicz

The centerpiece of this exhibit is a group of four angled shapes that support a strong signage element. A wash of light and diamond blocking separates each section of the modules. Aisle counters and peripheral structures pick up this unusual design, as does an element of the area used as background for live presentations.

**EXHIBITOR**
Beecham-Upjohn
**PRODUCER**
Dimension Works, Bensenville, IL
**DESIGNER**
Stan Muklewicz

**EXHIBITOR**
International Cable Technology
**PRODUCER**
KPW Productions, New York
**DESIGNER**
Picmai

Each of the eight circular rooms demonstrated a different type of music. Visitors were issued portable earphones which activated a low-power transmitter when the room was entered, thus preventing interference. The units used Octanorm elements.

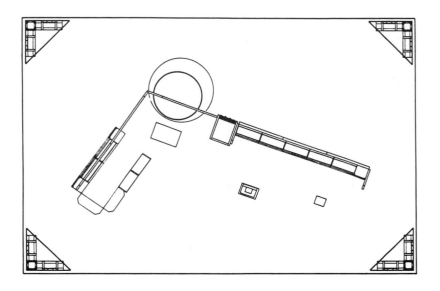

**EXHIBITOR**
W.R. Grace & Co.
**PRODUCER**
Giltspur Exhibits/Boston,
  Avon, MA
**DESIGNER**
John Barrett

To show how the exhibitor's products produced economies, a raised platform duplicated the exact size of columns used in a new Seattle high-rise tower. Placed on a circular piece of red carpet, it showed how much bigger the column would have been without the exhibitor's product. A programmable message repeater was used vertically in another demonstration showing the properties of the additive.

**EXHIBITOR**
Data Force
**PRODUCER**
Westberry Co.
**DESIGNER**
James Walker

A demonstration network was set up in this booth, with the connecting cables running in translucent red tubes overhead. Chaser lights indicated the flow of information. The Tech-Exhibit lightweight system was used.

**EXHIBITOR**
Wang
**PRODUCER**
Chicago Scenic Studios, Live
  Marketing (both Chicago, IL)
**DESIGNER**
Tom Ryan, R.D. Design Assoc.,
  Chicago, IL

The key element of this exhibit
was a 30' turntable on which a
75-member audience rode,
while viewing five separate
areas, at which two live
presenters told the product story.
The last of these areas utilized
three projection screens which
rolled up to reveal the exit.

# CHAPTER
# 7
# MUSEUMS

**EXHIBITORS**
Target, Hills Pet Products,
    DuPont, W.L. Gore
**PRODUCERS**
Haas Display Co., Berger Transfer
    (both) Minneapolis, MN
**DESIGNER**
Richard Giffin, Exhibit Design
    System

Housed in a custom-renovated
48-foot van, this traveling exhibit
tells the public about Antarctica
and the 1990 International Trans-
Arctica Expedition. It features a
sound system that plays
specially-made tapes of gusting
winds and howling dogs, a white
dropped ceiling and white
fiberglass walls. There is a
dramatic 24' diorama, complete
with life-sized mannequins of the
co-leaders of the expedition, two
dogs, a sled used on the
Greenland training run, a tent
and a ceiling-to-floor
photomural.

**EXHIBITOR**
Museum of Science & Industry,
    Chicago, IL
**PRODUCER**
Museum of Science & Industry
**DESIGNERS**
Grant Haring, Museum;
    Linda Buchanan, R.D. Design
    Associates, Chicago

An actor/musician uses music to explain the structure of DNA and how it works. Before an audience of about 100, as he plays a synthesizer, the appropriate monoliths in the background light up, adding a visual parallel to the explanation. The monoliths, each representing a different amino acid, also incorporate rear projection screens.

**EXHIBITOR**
Unisys
**PRODUCER**
Presentations South Inc.,
    Orlando, FL
**DESIGNER**
Robert J. McGarry

Installed on an existing curved
wall in EPCOT's Communicore,
this display offers a color photo
mounted on Sintra. The cut-out
jigsaw pieces, as well as the
demonstration counters, also use
Sintra.

**EXHIBITOR**
Johns Hopkins Hospital
**PRODUCER**
Adler Display Inc., Baltimore, MD
**DESIGNERS**
Ronald L. Adler,
    Lorena Llanes-Streb

A series of panels, carrying
documents and photographs,
were flexible enough to adapt to
a variety of locations. The same
panels were used to form display
cases for artifacts. The title panel
was reproduced in miniature on
each of the display panels, giving
a sense of unity.

**EXHIBITOR**
Anne Murray Centre
**PRODUCER**
J&O Exhibits Ltd.
**DESIGNER**
Jack Sheppard

This permanent environmental
exhibit covers over 3,500 square
feet. The drywall interior has
built-in showcases and
specialized lighting effects,
which include rear-lit graphics
through mirror surfaces,
animated and neon lighting, a
computerized sequentially-lit
costume exhibit, multi-monitor
audio-visuals, and a theater.

**EXHIBITOR**
Lawrence S. Givens Wildlife
   Interpretive Center,
   Huntsville, AL
**PRODUCER**
Wilderness Graphics Inc.,
   Tallahassee, FL
**DESIGNER**
R. Marvin Cook, Jr.

Located in an urban center, the Givens Center attracts many visitors to whom the concepts of wildlife management are new. Dioramas illustrate management activities throughout the year. An audio message with each diorama, augmented by text and graphics on panels, tells the story.

**EXHIBITOR**
Felsenthal National Wildlife
   Refuge, Crossett, AR
**PRODUCER**
Wilderness Graphics Inc.,
   Tallahassee, FL
**DESIGNER**
R. Marvin Cook, Jr.

In this display unit, an animated mannequin, dressed as an archeologist at an authentic excavation site, tells of the operation. Artifacts and transparencies are lighted in synchronization to give visitors an interesting perspective on the historic occupation of the area by native Americans.

**EXHIBITOR**
Arthur R. Marshall Loxahatchee
National Wildlife Refuge
**PRODUCER**
Wilderness Graphics Inc.,
Tallahassee, FL
**DESIGNER**
R. Marvin Cook, Jr.

Located on the northern edge of
the Everglades, this center
concentrates on the importance
of water in the area. The exhibits
utilize dioramas, photos, text,
graphics and audio messages.

**Everglades Managers**

**ARTHUR R. MARSHALL LOXAHATCHEE NATIONAL WILDLIFE REFUGE**

Arthur R. Marshall Loxahatchee National Wildlife Refuge comprises one of three huge freshwater storage areas built by the Army Corps of Engineers. To facilitate water storage and flood control, the South Florida Water Management District cooperates with the Corps to manage water levels.

levees and canals on the refuge. An agreement between the District and the U.S. Fish and Wildlife Service permitted establishment of the refuge in 1951. The refuge is challenged with protecting the fragile ecosystem that still exists in the northern Everglades.

**A REGIONAL ECOSYSTEM**

In satellite photographs, the pattern of the once vast Everglades ecosystem can be tracked. For the Everglades survival, rainfall that overflows from Lake Okeechobee and the northern drainages must flow southward to nourish the sawgrass, tree islands, and other plant communities on which

so many wildlife species depend, how an important part of this ecosystem, the adjacent urban and agricultural development is also dependent on the quality and quantity of the water in the Everglades. Managing for man and wildlife is the difficult mission of the Everglades managers.

# Shell Midden

# Burial Mound

**EXHIBITOR**
Spanish Point at the Oaks,
  Sarasota, FL
**PRODUCER**
Wilderness Graphics Inc.,
  Tallahassee, FL
**DESIGNER**
R. Marvin Cook, Jr.

Primarily designed for fourth-graders, this exhibit is part of the Sarasota County (FL) education program. It tells about archeology through an innovative cross-section model of a shell midden and burial mound. Interactive drawers and doors allow people to discover prepared artifacts. Other exhibits help children learn about the dress and food of Indians and early settlers. A chest, packed with 19th century artifacts, demonstrates what a pioneer family would bring to the area to start a new life. Students sing along with a reproduction pipe organ, to pioneer era songs played by a message repeatèr or electronic keyboard.

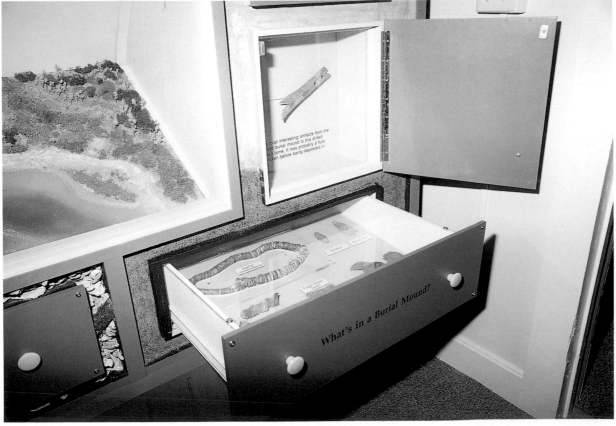

**EXHIBITOR**
The Travelers
**PRODUCER**
John Oldham Studios,
   Wethersfield, CT
**DESIGNERS**
James L. Colbert, Stephen Perez

The Travelers wanted an attention-getting, non-conservative exhibit to display the current NFL Man of the Year, and his 14 predecessors, at the Football Hall of Fame. Its dimensions were restricted to 8' x 8' x 2'. The current award winner's portrait was centered in the goal post at the end of a forced perspective view of a football field within a stadium. The trophy was spotlighted on the left side, with support graphics in a lightbox on the right. Smaller photos were lined up just under the main display. To see a short video about any winner, the visitor touched a flush-mounted membrane switch beneath the desired photo. This actuated a laser disc sequence. The computer, built into the cabinet, counted the number of times each button was pushed. Because of its heavy use—about 20,000 visitors a year—durability and accessibility were important characteristics. All elements could be serviced from the front of the unit.

**EXHIBITOR**
Mayo Clinic, Rochester, MN
**PRODUCERS**
various
**DESIGNERS**
Malcolm Grear Designers;
    Mayo Environmental Design*

The exhibit at the Mayo Clinic is designed to recognize its many benefactors, as well as to house rotating exhibits of art and artifacts related to the Clinic. It occupies 1,860 square feet in a space adjacent to a three-story atrium. The names of benefactors are carved into slate strips, with the letters filled with color. They are mounted in teakwood tracks which allow names to be added wherever they fit alphabetically. Illumination is by hidden down-wash lighting. The art and artifacts are exhibited in internally-illuminated, wall-mounted exhibit cases, as well as in free-standing exhibit cases which are lit from above with an imbedded track lighting system. There are also expandable and retractable free-standing wall systems for displaying two-dimensional art.

**EXHIBITOR**
Mayo Clinic, Scottsdale, AZ
**PRODUCER**
Giltspur Exhibits/Boston,
    Avon, MA
**DESIGNER**
Malcolm Grear Designers,
    Providence, RI

The last of three exhibits at
Mayo Clinic highlighted the
historical achievements of the
organization, reported on its
recent developments, and
looked ahead to the future. It
ended with a message of
participation for the viewer. The
exhibit covered two walls, one
29' 5¾'' and the other 34'
10¾'', both 8' 3¾'' high. An
artificial wall, one-foot thick,
accommodated the assorted light
fixtures and the dimensional light
boxes. The wooden structure
was surfaced with a colored
Nevamor finish. Major copy
appeared as transparencies,
while photo captions were
silkscreened onto dimensional
blocks, illuminated by openings
in the light boxes holding the
color transparencies.

**EXHIBITOR**
National Baseball Hall of Fame
**PRODUCER**
Maltbie Associates, Mt. Laurel, NJ
**DESIGNER**
William Kissiloff, Kissiloff
    Associates, New York

The challenge of the new East
wing was to incorporate an
adjacent gymnasium building, no
longer in use. The open alley
space between the old gym and
the existing museum provided
transportation on escalators to
the second floor, which was
enclosed with a glass-covered
roof truss. The interior space
utilized the visual vocabulary of
the game, consisting of high
color graphics and banners,
special flooring and finishes, and
appropriate exhibit treatments
under railed balconies that
resulted in dramatic effects. The
entire environment simulated the
ambience of the ball park, and
projected the theme of the new
wing, "Baseball Today."
Included is specially
commissioned sculptural artwork
of fans, which surrounds the
visitors on ramps leading to a
200-seat multi-media
presentation in a stadium-like
theater.

**EXHIBITOR**
Barclay's Bank of North America
**PRODUCER**
Giltspur Exhibits/Boston,
  Avon, MA

When Barclay's was in process of building its new American headquarters at 75 Wall St., a great many artifacts from the early days were discovered. It was thus decided to build a museum to show these and to tell the history of Wall St. between 1690 and 1820. The design concept was to move the viewer through a visual archeological search. A flexible, modular system contained transparencies and held artifacts, light boxes and text panels.

**EXHIBITOR**
Museum of Fine Arts of the
    Rhode Island School of Design
**PRODUCER**
Exhibition Department of the
    Museum
**DESIGNER**
Robert Segal, Segaldesign,
    Arlington, MA

The subject of the show was daily life in ancient Coptic Egypt. The challenge was to unify a large collection of objects, widely diverse in subject matter and media, into an intriguing visitor experience. The desert chapel reconstruction at the far end of the gallery provided a visual focal point, from which emanated Coptic liturgical music, setting the tone for the entire exhibit.

# CHAPTER

## 8

# TOO GOOD
# TO LEAVE
# OUT

**EXHIBITOR**
Fisher-Price
**PRODUCER**
Design for Industry, Buffalo, NY
**DESIGNERS**
Andrea Billias, Greg Meadows,
   Tim Dexter, Tamara Dowd,
   Jack Snyder

Over 30,000 square feet of showroom space, located on two floors of an office building in midtown Manhattan, showcased a diverse product line. Fifteen product environments were developed for the lines shown in that space. For example, the Crib & Playpen toy line used giant toy blocks as product pedestals, while marble columns and pediments reinforced the concept of learning behind the Fun Starters, a toy line developed around education.

**EXHIBITOR**
American Academy of
    Dermatology & Ortho
    Pharmaceutical Corp.
**PRODUCER**
Spaeth Design, New York, NY
**DESIGNER**
Michael Meister

This unusual project, designed to teach consumers that today's tan is tomorrow's wrinkle, was planned to travel to major shopping malls across the country. The focal point of the presentation was a mini-theater with two three-dimensional, computer-controlled, cartoon-like characters. They talked to the audience about the dangers of too much sun, how to protect yourself from sun damage, and how to treat sun-damaged skin. In the opposite side of this structure was a facsimile of a movie theater entrance, complete with marquee, ticket booth, and animatronic cashier. Posters stressing safety points, in the form of movie posters, supported the message. In another unit, people from the audience were asked to participate in a television game show. Other interaction was offered by two dioramas.

223

**EXHIBITOR**
AT&T Network Systems
**PRODUCER**
Murphy & Orr Co.,
    Forest Park, GA
**DESIGNER**
George Stough, Stough & William
    Design Consultants

For a training facility that had to be used in many locations around the country, the interior of a 48' van was fitted with display panels and demonstration devices. Folding tables, graphics with many mounted products, and a slide and video area were included. In the front was an 800-pound switching unit standing over 6' high and 4' wide. It was hinged to the wall for access to the driver's area. Backlit duratrans line the walls between the product panels.

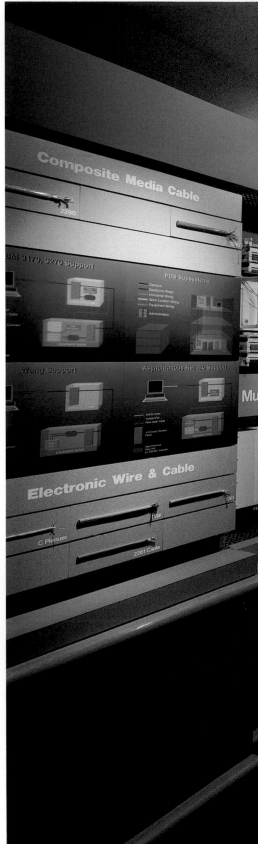

**EXHIBITOR**
ASICS
**PRODUCER**
Display Works, Irvine, CA
**DESIGNERS**
Carter W. Lee; vignette panels by
    John Bueck

This exterior wall display set the mood for a trade show. The entire wall is Impac wiregrid on bases, with Zolatoned sporting equipment.

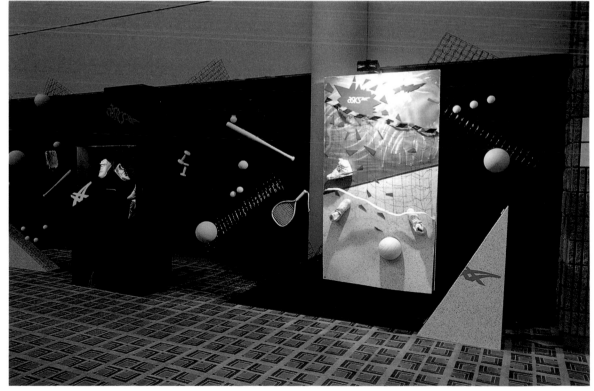

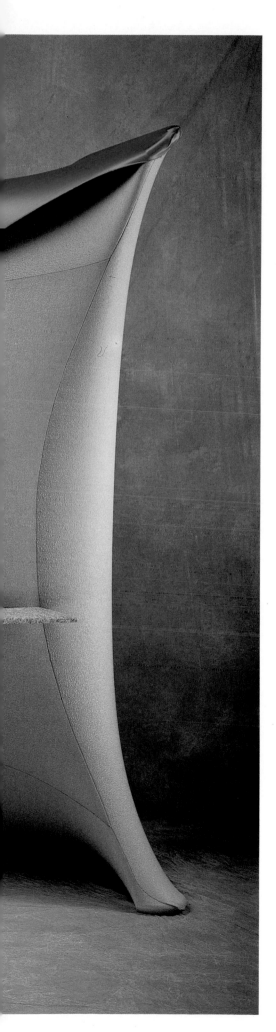

**EXHIBITOR**
Panelglide
**PRODUCER**
Panelglide, Chicago, IL
**DESIGNERS**
Cindy Thompson, Charles Bryant,
Herb Velasquez, Patrick Spatz

This unusual tension fabric technique can be used to produce very lightweight backgrounds and furniture. A loop fabric stretches over durable aluminum sections.

**EXHIBITOR**
Maryland Department of Tourism
**PRODUCER**
Adler Display Inc., Baltimore, MD
**DESIGNER**
Ronald L. Adler

At night, when the Information Center is not staffed, roll-away cabinets serve as doors which have racks of literature available to the public.

**EXHIBITOR**
Southland Mall, Hayward, CA
**PRODUCER**
T.L. Horton Design Inc.,
    Dallas, TX
**DESIGNER**
Tony Horton

The shopping mall wanted to call special attention, and draw traffic to, a lower level area that was dedicated to a variety of food outlets. Brightly-colored 16' arched entries were highly visible and drew shoppers into the lower court. A brightly-colored mobile of 8' pieces of foam, cut in shapes of food, was suspended from the 40' ceiling with aircraft wire. A 16' signage marquee, with 150' of red ribbon fabricated from bent metal, defined the stage area used for special events.

**EXHIBITOR**
Design Management Institute;
Harvard Business School
**PRODUCER**
Giltspur Exhibit/Boston,
    Avon, MA
**DESIGNERS**
Jane Corbus, Jeff Crewe,
    Peggy Kirk, Giltspur;
    Chris Pullman, WGBH Design

The exhibit is designed to travel for two years, in the United States and then in Europe, acquainting the business public with an understanding of industrial design as a process. The exhibit has two distinct parts, one covering the process of design, the other showing case studies of individual products. The case studies are presented on free-standing kiosks, while process line is created from 70 panels placed in an undulating arrangement corresponding to the complex, non-linear nature of the design process. The process line uses a custom system, based on a pre-painted panel which supports itself with the addition of a laminated plywood shelf and tubular metal leg. Tambour strips are velcro-connected to make the line a complete unit. A single 150-watt halogen stem light illuminates the graphics.

**EXHIBITOR**
Olin/Winchester
**PRODUCER**
Pingel Displays Inc., St. Louis, MO
**DESIGNERS**
Bob Meyer, Steve Carrow

A pre-fabricated metal building was transformed into an elegant exhibit. The interior elements were all built at the shop and installed on site. Graphic alcoves were covered with loop nylon for easy changes, with down lighting for good visibility. A large screen monitor was built in. Polished brass and bright red are used throughout. Outside, a vinyl canopy and a raised, lighted sign called attention to the exhibit.

**EXHIBITOR**
Cray Research
**PRODUCER**
Haas Display Co.,
    Minneapolis, MN
**DESIGNER**
Richard Giffin, Exhibit Design
    System

For an exhibit originally intended
for the Senate Office Building, a
full-scale model of a
supercomputer was made of
wood.

**EXHIBITOR**
**NYNEX**
**PRODUCER**
Denby Associates, Princeton, NJ
**DESIGNER**
Tony Lualdi

In the lobby outside the auditorium in which the annual shareholders' meeting was held, this exhibit tells the company's five-year history on a series of towers ranging from 12' to 24' in height. Information kiosks and a refreshment area complete the installation.

**EXHIBITOR**
Delsey Luggage
**PRODUCER**
Adler Display, Baltimore, MD
**DESIGNERS**
Ronald Adler,
  Lorena Llanes-Streb

This unusual display podium has a cross-section that matches the company logo. Internal fluorescent lights produce a red glow between the levels of the segmented platform. A space for a television monitor or a small display window is incorporated into the tallest segment.

**EXHIBITOR**
Monsanto/Detergent Division
**PRODUCER**
The Robert Falk Group,
St. Louis, MO
**DESIGNERS**
Robert J. Falk, Jr.,
Gretchen Schisla

This traveling presentation was designed to set up in a single day in ordinary hotel conference rooms. It is a portable stage system with seven displays and multiple print materials. The staging provides a rear projection screen.

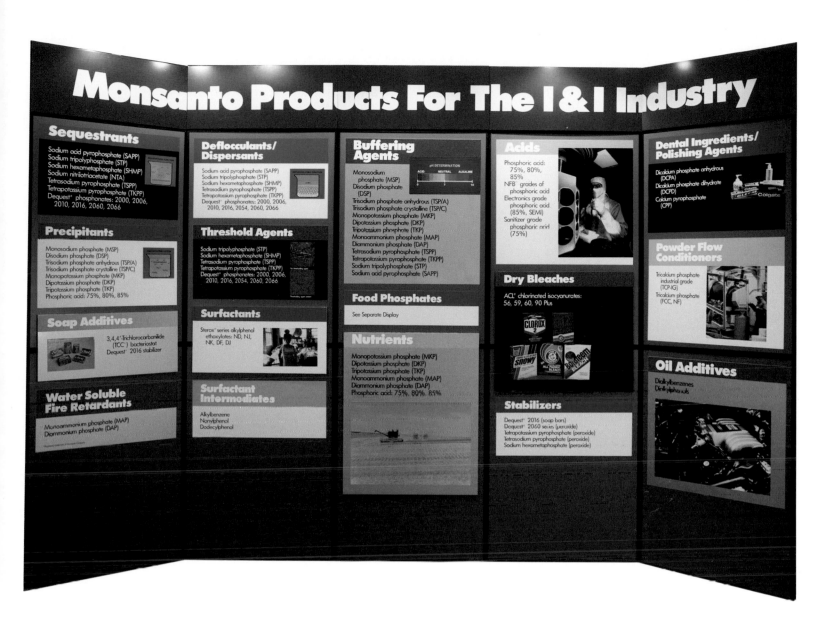

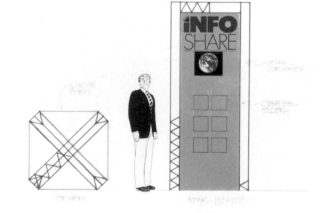

**EXHIBITOR**
Porsche Cars(GB) Ltd.
**PRODUCER**
Newton Display Group Ltd.,
    Manchester, UK
**DESIGNER**
Furneaux Stewart

The stand features 8 Porsche automobiles, each mounted on an individual rotating disc. Each disc independently revolved, stopped and started, reversed, and changed its angle from 15 to 35°, creating a fluid, floating, moving image. Theatrical lighting, mounted on the top of the towers, highlighted the individual cars. Lights were also fixed to the base of the discs, creating images on the back walls.

**EXHIBITOR**
Bloomingdale's
**PRODUCER**
Model Builders Inc., Chicago, IL
**DESIGNER**
Not available

This replica of the Eiffel Tower
was installed in the Chicago
store for a six-week production.
Standing 43'3" tall, the structure
was made of glue-laminated
beams and other wood
elements. It was made of 47 pre-
fabricated sections, screwed
together during assembly.
Installation involved four people
over a 10-hour period.

**EXHIBITOR**
Donohoe O'Brien & Co.
**PRODUCER**
T.L. Horton Design Inc.
**DESIGNER**
Tony Horton

Tying in with the company's advertising slogan, ''Generating Power,'' the identity signage for this exhibit was made of brightly colored foam gears which were turned by a small motor. Other gears carried the theme to all parts of the exhibit.

**EXHIBITOR**
Hercules
**PRODUCER**
Gordon Murray Design,
   Walnut Creek, CA
**DESIGNER**
Gordon Murray

Because the exhibitor attends
only one show each year, and
does not want to present the
same image over a long period,
it wanted construction that was
disposable. Everything in the
photo, except the Eyebeam™
metal frames, was fabricated
from foam and assembled with
epoxy. The pieces were
demolished after the show!

# Index of Exhibitors

## A

Advo System Inc. *52*
Allen and Hanbury's *222*
Alside *107*
American Academy of Dermatology *222*
Amoco Chemical Co. *134*
Amoco Performance Products *110*
Anacomp *175*
Anne Murray Centre *188*
Ansell-Americas/Medical Division *80*
Architectural Walls Ltd. *52*
Art-Craft Optical Co. *35*
Artesian Industries *81*
Arthur R. Marshall Loxahatchee National
  Wildlife Refuge *191*
ASICS *227*
AT&T Network Systems *224*
Avant Garde Optics *63*
Aviall *72*

## B

Barclay's Bank of North America *202*
Bauerfeind *74*
Bearings Inc. *38*
Beecham Labs *67*
Beecham-Upjohn *178*
Bell & Howell *104*
Black & Decker *87*
Bloomingdale's *245*
Borden Foods *101*
Burger King Corporation *100*

## C

Cafaro Co., The *119*
Canyon Products *41*
Caribbean Lumber Co. *36*
Cessna *125*
Champion Products Inc. *154*
Chips *90*
Code-A-Phone *151*
ConAgra *106*
Cooper Rolls *150*
Crane/National Vendors *172*
Cray Research *236*

## D

Dainippon Screen *174*
Data Force *181*
Delsey Luggage *238*
Denby Associates' *77*
Design Management Institute *234*
Diagraph Corporation *158*
Dickinson/Lost Acres *46*
Diebold *116*
Dimension Works Inc. *44*
Donohoe O'Brien & Co. *246*
Duncan Aviation *56*
Dupli-Color Products Co. *153*
DuPont/Automotive *121*
DuPont/Electronic *118*
Duracell USA *176*
Dynatech *128*

## E

Ecolab, Int'l Division *19*
Emco Industries *70*

Equity Properties & Development Co. *132*
Evans & Sutherland *58*
EZ Paintr Corp. *143*

## F

Felsenthal National Wildlife Refuge *190*
Ferretti *82*
Fisher-Price *208*
Fitness Quest *40*
Focusrite *18*
Fujitsu Inc. of America *129*

## G

GMC Truck Division *123*
Government of Singapore *115*
W.R. Grace & Co. *180*

## H

Hamilton Beach *177*
Hartmann Luggage *115*
Hattori Corp. *140*
HBO & Co. *22*
Hercules *248*
Hewlett-Packard *144, 171*
Hitachi *132*
Hobart Inc. *148*
Honeywell/Building Controls Division *161*
Honeywell/Residential *144, 173*
Husky Injection Molding Systems *149*

## I

ICI Baquacil *74*
Inland Steel *30*
Intelligent Business Systems *167*
Inter-Continental Hotels *25*

## J

J.M. Pedreira & Son Inc. *17*
Jacobs Suchard Canada *162*
Jerry Madison Jewelry *33*
Johns Hopkins Hospital *187*

## K

Kaltenbach & Voigt & Co. *99*
Kangaroos USA *97*
Karp's Bakery Products *48*
Keller Tool *87*
Kitzing Inc. *55*
Kodak Health Sciences *141*
Konami *109*
Konover Associates *91*

## L

L.J. Hooker Developments *137*
LaSalle Partners *96*
Lawrence S. Givens Wildlife Interpretive
  Center *190*
Legend Sporting Goods *161*
Lehndorff Property Management *95*
Lucas Avitron *73*

## M

Magicsilk *130*
Maglo Products *75*
Mannington Mills Inc. *68*
Marine Midland Automotive Finance Corp.
  *64*
Maryland Dept. of Tourism *231*
Masco Corp. *124*
Mayo Clinics *196, 197*
McGard *23*
Mead Johnson Pharmaceuticals *159*
Medtronic *102*
Metagus *89*
Mitsubishi *169*
Metal Leve *48*
Miller Fluid Power *111*
MMS International *142*
Monsanto *42*
Monsanto/Detergent Division *239*
Morgan Doors *28*
Murphy & Orr Co. *15*
Museum of Fine Arts of the Rhode Island
  School of Design *203*
Museum of Science & Industry *186*

## N

National Baseball Hall of Fame *199*
Navistar Int'l *122*
NEC *138*
NEC America *97*
Nichols-Homeshield *24*
NYNEX Corp. *236*

## O

Olin/Winchester *235*
Oneida *95*
Oshkosh Truck *101*

## P

Panelglide *229*
Penn Racquet Sports *51*
Pierce & Stevens Corp. *54*
Pontiac Motor Division, General Motors *120*
Porsche Cars (GB) Ltd. *243*
Pueringer Distributing Inc. *39*
Pure Data *55*

## Q

Quaker Food Service *153*

## R

Rampart Packaging *47*
Rasna *49*
Raymond Weil *152*
RCA Records, Country Music Division *32*
Reader's Digest *29*
Redkin Hair Products *40*
Regal Ware Inc. *23*
Reggie's Wax *27*
Relational Technology Inc. *60*
Rochester Instrument Systems *24*
Rodem Co. *18*
Rofin Sinar *65*

# Index of Producers

## S

S & W  78
Sandoz Pharmaceutical/Schering-Plough  86, 88
Sandridge Gourmet  28
Santander Federal Savings Bank  36
Seagil Software  50
Seiko Instruments  46
Serono Laboratories  76
Sidbec Dosco  84
Simitar Entertainment Inc.  163
Singapore Defense Industries  148
Singapore Tourist Promotion Board  147
Singer Sewing Machine Co.  157
Snapper Lawnmower  108
Sony-Cetek Inc.  34
South Central Bell  31
Southland Mall  232
Southwestern Bell Telephone  62
Spanish Point at the Oaks  193
Sterling Plumbing Group  112

## T

I-Fal Corp.  8
Target  185
Taurus Int'l  17
Teradyne Connection Systems  170
Terumo Corp.  20
Thermador/Waste King  79
Toshiba ISD  146
Travelers, The  195

## U

Unisys  187
United Exposition Service  67
Universal Motors  39

## V

Valmet Paper Machinery  165
Vestron Television  85
Viacom Enterprises  127
Victoreen Inc.  78
Video Treasures  82
Virgin Atlantic Airways  43
VPI  177

## W

W.A. Lane Inc.  37
Wagner/Belden  21
Walt Disney Co.  71
Wang  169, 182
Watson Bowman Acme  16
Westwood  105
Williams, Jackson, Ewing  26

## Z

Zenith Data Systems  139

## A

ABF Industries  38
Adler Display Inc.  26, 187, 231, 238
Advanced Exhibit Methods  162
Alley Shop, The  18
Atlanta Display Mart  50

## B

Beyond Exhibits Inc.  47
Bluepeter  56, 60

## C

Chicago Scenic Studios  168, 182
Color & Design Exhibits Inc.  46, 90, 128
Communication Exhibits Inc.  78, 81, 82, 116, 150
Convention Exhibits Inc.  25, 75, 112
Cyclonics Inc.  48, 51, 87, 107, 110, 134, 142

## D

Davis Design Associates  76, 171
Denby Associates  74, 77, 237
Design Center, The  125, 127
Design for Industry  16, 20, 54, 105
Design South Inc.  22, 79, 102
Dimension Works Inc.  18, 44, 48, 67, 78, 101, 109, 148, 153, 174, 178
Dimensional Studios Inc.  118, 121
Displaycraft Inc.  122
Display Shop, The  39, 46, 165
Display Works  227

## E

Escaparates Inc.  17, 36
Exhibitgroup Atlanta  36, 68, 74, 106, 130
Exhibitgroup Chicago  123
Exhibitgroup San Francisco  49, 65
Exhibit by Design  104, 139, 175
Exhibit Systems of California  37, 40
Exhibition Dept. of Museum of Fine Arts of the Rhode Island School of Design  203

## F

Fahey Exhibits  170
Fairconsult GmbH  99
Freeman Exhibit Co.  71, 97

## G

Giltspur/Boston  86, 88, 158, 180, 197, 202, 234
Giltspur Exhibits/Rochester  23, 43, 95, 132
Gordon Murray Design  248
Greyhound Exposition Services  119

## H

Haas Display Co.  64, 144, 160, 163, 173, 185, 236
Hartwig Exhibitions  28, 52, 101, 176, 177
Herb Dixon & Associates  70

## J

J & O Exhibits  55, 188
Joan Carol Design and Exhibit Group  28
John Oldham Studios  34, 52, 91, 141, 167, 195

## K

Kadoke Display Ltd.  82, 95, 115, 138, 146
Kitzing Inc.  19, 21, 30, 55, 97, 111, 124, 149, 153
KMK Industries Inc.  23, 80, 83, 143
KPW Productions  33, 152

## L

Lewellen & Best  151
Les Concepts Polystand Inc.  84
Lynch Exhibits  140

## M

Maltbie Associates  199
Model Builders Inc.  245
Murphy & Orr Co.  31, 224
Museum of Science & Industry  186

## N

Newton Display Group Ltd.  144, 243

## O

Ontario Design Inc.  224, 35, 154

## P

Panelglide  229
Pico Art Int'l Pte. Ltd.  147
Pingel Displays Inc.  62, 87, 158, 172, 235
Presentations South Inc.  17, 187
Promotional Fixtures Inc.  38

## R

Rave Reviews  129
Robert Falk Group, The  42, 239
Rogers Displays  27
Rowe Thomas Display Co.  120

## S

Spaeth Design  222

## T

1220 Exhibits Inc.  29, 32, 85, 108, 115, 156
T.L. Horton Design Inc.  96, 100, 132, 136, 232, 246
Technical Exhibits Corp.  161

## U

United Longchamp Int'l.  63, 89, 169

## W

Westberry Co.  181
Wilderness Graphics Inc.  190, 191
Windsor Exhibits Inc.  24

# Index of Designers

## A

Adell, Shelton  *119*
Adelman, Corey  *122*
Adler, Ronald L.  *26, 187, 231, 238*
Artzt, Gary  *72*

## B

Baltus, Baudouin  *63, 66, 168*
Baridon, Jim  *71*
Barrett, John  *86, 88, 158, 180*
Beetlestone, Jayne  *49, 65*
Billias, Andrea  *20, 105*
Broberg, Jerry  *38*
Bryant, Charles  *229*
Buchanan, Linda  *168, 186*
Burke, Jeffrey  *104, 139, 174*
Burns, Mark S.  *36, 68, 74*
Burns, Susan  *50*

## C

Cameron, Tom  *129*
Carder, Larry  *40*
Carlson, Joanne  *164*
Carrow, Steve  *235*
Colbert, James L.  *34, 166, 195*
Cook, Jr., R. Marvin  *190, 191*
Corbus, Jane  *234*
Corke, Derek  *148*
Crawley, Jacqueline  *146*
Crewe, Jeff  *234*
Crouch, Ray  *132*

## D

Davis, John M.  *76, 171*
Dexter, Tim  *20, 54, 105*
Dixon, Herb  *70*
Dowd, Tamara  *105*
Dunaj, Cynthia  *153*

## E

Edwards, Michael  *106*
Ense, Ludwig  *98*
Epperson, Alane  *28*
Falk, Jr., Robert J.  *42, 239*
Finn, Thomas  *24, 35, 154*
Fornes, Jeanne  *95*
Fraser, Jean  *84*
Freedom Design Group  *174*

## G

Gallagher, James  *24*
Gamble, Keith L.  *38*
Giambrone, David  *161*
Giffin, Richard  *64, 144, 160, 163, 173, 184, 236*
Godbout, Charles  *84*
Gotschall, Ernie  *82*
Grant Haring Museum  *186, 187*

## H

Haas, Dirk  *43*
Han, A.M.  *162*
Hanlon, James  *30, 97, 111, 124*
Harrison, Steven  *42*
Harshfield, Curtis  *125*
Hatter, Barry  *18*
Hejka, Jack  *37*
Hess, Andy  *80, 83*
Hoffmockel, Bill  *18, 44, 78*
Holman, Tom  *17*
Horn, Jon  *39*
Horton, Tony  *96, 100, 132, 136, 232, 246*

## J

Jeffries, David  *41, 78*

## K

Katzowitz, Joel  *22, 29*
Kek, Cheng Eng  *148*
Keller, John  *112*
Kemble, Susan  *48, 108, 153*
Kirk, Peggy  *234*
Kissiloff, William  *199*
Kitzing, Fred  *30, 55, 124*
Klym, Michael  *94*
Kingsmen Designers & Producers  *115*

## L

L'Esperance, Guy  *27*
Lee, Babbe  *89*
Lee, Carter W.  *227*
Lewis, Rick  *123*
Llanes-Streb, Lorena  *187, 238*
Lualdi, Tony  *74, 237*
Lutz, Wil  *63, 87, 158*
Lyons, G.P.  *28, 52, 101, 176, 177*

## M

MacQuarrie, Karen  *82*
Manga, Vito  *146*
Mauk, Mitchell  *56, 60*
Mayer, Scott  *26*
McGarry, Robert  *17, 187*
Meadows, Greg  *16, 20, 105*
Meagher, Mark  *32*
Meister, Michael  *222*
Meyer, Bob  *172, 235*
Montgomery, Lisa  *77*
Mothes, Rusty  *46*
Muklewicz, Stan  *67, 148, 178*
Murray, Gordon  *248*

## N

Nieves, Wanda I.  *17, 36*

## O

O'Farrell, Claire  *85, 115*
Owen, Miriam  *29, 108, 156*

## P

Panzarella, Joe  *149*
Perez, Stephen  *141, 195*
Picmai  *33, 152*
Pullman, Chris  *234*

## R

Raflo, Jeff  *14*
Reckeweg, Don  *140*
Reese, Jack  *25*
Rich, Rudy  *72*
Rizzini, Ricard o  *48*
Roberson, Gina  *51, 107, 134, 142*
Ryan, Teddie Jo  *47*
Ryan, Tom  *182*

## S

Santarelli, Anthony  *142*
Saubert, Michael  *25*
Saunders, Scott  *102*
Schisla, Gretchen  *239*
Schowalter, Tom  *101*
Segal, Robert  *170, 203*
Sereduke, John M.  *118, 121*
Sheppard, Jack  *188*
Snyder, Jack  *16, 20, 54, 105*
Spatz, Patrick  *229*
Sicuzza, Martin (Marty)  *51, 87, 107, 110, 134, 142*
Stahlberg, Paul,  *151*
Stewart Furneaux  *144, 243*
Stewart, Gary  *102*
Stone, Stuart  *120*
Stough, George  *31, 224*
Suddick, Debbie  *55*

## T

Teager, John  *138, 146*
Thompson, Cindy  *229*

## U

Uzarowski, David  *23*

## V

Vargas, Ben  *19, 21*
Velasquez, Herb  *229*

## W

Walker, Jim  *181*
Walsh, Stephen  *52, 91, 141*
Walters, Brian  *40, 81, 116, 150*
Wegner, Jack  *23, 80, 83, 143*
Wilson, Bill  *172*
Wycislak, Matthew  *112*

## Y

Yurkin, Tom  *97*

# POINT OF PURCHASE DESIGN 2

POINT OF PURCHASE DESIGN 2 is the most comprehensive sourcebook for designers and users of point-of-purchase advertising materials. These displays have emerged as one of the most varied, creative, and vital dimensions of retail advertising and merchandising. A sequel to PBC's immensely successful first book on point-of-purchase, this volume includes all the latest developments in design and use of this sales tool.

Studies show that 60 to 65 percent of purchase decisions are made in the store at the time of purchase. The items in these outlets are often small and lower-priced, but point-of-purchase strategies have also proved successful for marketing bigger, more expensive items for which the consumer needs extensive technical information, such as cars, major appliances and banking services. In addition, marketing strategies are shifting from image-driven to impact-driven, thus increasing the use and development of point-of-purchase design.

Each chapter explores a category of related goods and opens with a trend analysis of that category. Included are:

- Food and paper goods
- Transportation
- Beverages
- Household Goods
- Hardware/Building materials
- Farm, agriculture and garden supplies
- Health and beauty aids
- Services

**FOR ORDER INFORMATION PLEASE SEE ORDER FORM ON THE BACK JACKET.**

256 pages, 9" x 12"
Over 300 illustrations
ISBN 0-86636-074-3
$60.00

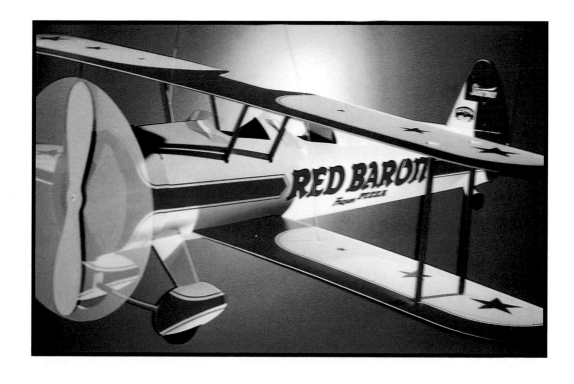

# CLIO AWARDS
# 30 YEARS OF ADVERTISING EXCELLENCE
## 1960-1989

**A LAVISH 9″ x 12″
FULL COLOR, 496 PAGE
HARDCOVER SALUTE TO
ADVERTISING EXCELLENCE.**

The most historical volume on the world of advertising ever published. This collector's edition features the storyboards, scripts and ads from the best U.S. and international campaigns for the past three decades in television/cinema, radio and print; along with all of the U.S. and international 1989 CLIO winners in the areas of television/Cinema, Cable, Radio, Print, Package Design and Specialty Advertising.

In addition to 30 years of award-winning advertisements, the book includes the reflections of the past chairmen of the CLIO Advisory Board, on the advertising industry.

A most comprehensive collection of the best in creativity, it should be of compelling interest to all, from the advertising executive to the client and consumer.

**FOR ORDER INFORMATION
PLEASE SEE ORDER FORM ON
THE BACK JACKET.**

496 pages, 9″ x 12″
Over 800 illustrations
ISBN 0-86636-115-4
$75.00

Official ball of the 1988 French Open.

# DIRECT MARKETING DESIGN

DIRECT MARKETING DESIGN illustrates award-winning advertising from the prestigious John Caples Award Program—one of the direct response industry's most coveted competition awards. Large, full-color photographs prominently display response, and detailed photographs focus on individual elements—envelopes, boxes, posters, stuffers, and other components.

Essays from the leading practitioners of direct marketing introduce each section and share their insights on the emerging trends in this exploding field of advertising. Accompanying each illustration is information that explains the purpose of the piece, details production aspects, and sales results. Also provided are credits for the agency, the client, the designer, the art director, and the copywriter.

The entire spectrum of direct response advertising is represented in this volume. Pieces are grouped by category covering the numerous uses of direct marketing:

- Direct Mail to Businesses
- Direct Mail to Consumers
- Direct Mail Catalogs
- Collateral Material
- Direct Response Campaigns, Multimedia
- Direct Response Campaigns, Single Medium
- Television Response Ads

DIRECT MARKETING DESIGN is a large-format, 9" x 12" hardbound idea book with 256 full-color pages. No designer, no advertising agency, no business involved in direct marketing can afford to be without this collection, destined to become a standard reference work for the industry.

FOR ORDER INFORMATION PLEASE SEE ORDER FORM ON THE BACK JACKET.

256 pages, 9" x 12"
Over 300 illustrations
ISBN 0-86636-006-9
$55.00 SALE PRICE $44.00

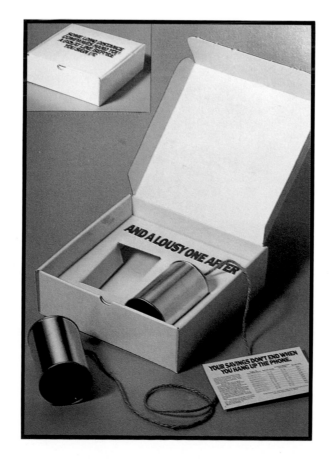

# DIRECT MARKETING DESIGN 2

DIRECT MARKETING DESIGN 2 vividly displays the newest ideas and techniques of the direct mail industry. In 248 full-color pages, the winners of the prestigious John Caples Awards are clearly presented. This competition is sponsored by the Direct Marketing Creative Guild, and is judged by a panel of direct marketing experts from all levels of the industry. Brief descriptions that include the designers' intent accompany each of the 270 illustrations. DIRECT MARKETING DESIGN 2 is a fabulous reference tool to all in the fields of direct mail, advertising, public relations and marketing. Many topics graphically present excellence in direct marketing creativity and design including:

- Direct mail for consumers
- Direct mail for business to business
- Print advertising for consumers and business-to-business
- Collateral Material
- Multimedia and single media direct response campaigns

248 pages, 9″ x 12″
Over 300 illustrations
ISBN 0-86636-061-1
$60.00

Hundreds of award-winning designs fill the 248 pages of this 9″ x 12″ idea sourcebook. Captions and chapter openers accompany the direct mail pieces and describe what is the special facet, that unique "something" that makes each piece a winner!

STAND OUT FROM THE REST. ORDER YOUR COPY TODAY!

**FOR ORDER INFORMATION PLEASE SEE ORDER FORM ON THE BACK JACKET.**